T0384218

Project Cost Recording and Reporting

Communication is a vital part of project management, and reports are one of the preferred vehicles for transmitting information to an intended internal or external audience. Reports are also part of the system of control and governance on projects, used to bring attention to issues and prompt action to improve project outcomes. There are countless ways of combining project information for consumption by stakeholders.

This book discusses the purpose of project reports, and provides examples of the format, content, timing, and audience for various types. Using principles of stakeholders and risk management, it presents a rationale for communication plans, enabling appropriate reporting at the project, program, and portfolio level. The author also:

- Presents tangible experience and suggestions for developing project reports.
- Discusses project reports in context, as applicable to types of stakeholders and the project lifecycle.
- Identifies sources and types of data required for adequate reporting.
- Offers examples of report formats, graphics, and content.
- Reflects on typical challenges encountered with project reporting.

It is essential reading for practitioners and students of project management, cost control, and accountancy.

Alexia Nalewaik is a professor of project management and sole practitioner consultant, the owner of QS Requin Corporation. She has over 25 years of experience in audit, systemic risk, project analytics, governance, and cost engineering. Alexia is Research Chair of the International Cost Engineering Council (ICEC). She is a Fellow of RICS Americas, AACE International, the Guild of Project Controls, and ICEC. She is a Past President of AACE International, and a Past Chair of ICEC. She is also a member of the American Society of Civil Engineers, IPMA-USA, and the National Association of Construction Auditors.

"Alexia reveals the power of data and analytics for project reporting in her new book. *Project Cost Recording and Reporting* reveals the underpinnings of project reporting for stakeholders that project, program and portfolio managers can leverage – communication, transparency and decisions that form project outcomes. I highly recommend this as a guidebook for project leaders working in a matrix or projectized organization."

Naomi Caietti, *Author, Founder and Director, Naomi Caietti Consulting, USA*

"The phrase 'the more things change, the more they remain the same' ('plus ça change, plus c'est la même chose'), was coined by French critic, journalist and novelist Jean-Baptiste Alphonse Karr (1808–1890) rings more true today than ever before. Alexia provides a comprehensive and thorough view in emphasizing the importance of accurate, unbiased and honest project reporting in her new book, *Project Cost Recording and Reporting*. In our current age of disruption, and the necessity for almost instantaneous decision-making, the need for robust project reporting is more important than ever before – as it always has been. For all practitioners of total cost management, this book is an essential guide and tool to getting project reporting right the first time."

Louise M. Vlatko, *Co-Founder and Director, Xmirus Pty Ltd, Australia*

Project Cost Recording and Reporting

Alexia Nalewaik

Routledge
Taylor & Francis Group

LONDON AND NEW YORK

First published 2020
by Routledge
2 Park Square, Milton Park, Abingdon, Oxon OX14 4RN

and by Routledge
52 Vanderbilt Avenue, New York, NY 10017

Routledge is an imprint of the Taylor & Francis Group, an informa business

© 2020 Alexia Nalewaik

The right of Alexia Nalewaik to be identified as author of this work
has been asserted by her in accordance with sections 77 and 78 of
the Copyright, Designs and Patents Act 1988.

British Library Cataloguing-in-Publication Data
A catalogue record for this book is available from the British Library

Library of Congress Cataloging-in-Publication Data
Names: Nalewaik, Alexia, 1968– author.
Title: Project cost recording and reporting / Alexia Nalewaik.
Description: Milton Park, Abingdon, Oxon ; New York, NY :
Routledge, 2020. | Includes bibliographical references and index.
Identifiers: LCCN 2019036490 (print) | LCCN 2019036491 (ebook) |
ISBN 9781409450993 (hardback) | ISBN 9781003001553 (ebook)
Subjects: LCSH: Project management. | Business report writing. |
Budget process.
Classification: LCC HD69.P75 N36 2020 (print) | LCC HD69.P75
(ebook) | DDC 658.4/04–dc23
LC record available at https://lccn.loc.gov/2019036490
LC ebook record available at https://lccn.loc.gov/2019036491

ISBN: 978-1-4094-5099-3 (hbk)
ISBN: 978-1-003-00155-3 (ebk)

Typeset in Times New Roman
by Wearset Ltd, Boldon, Tyne and Wear

Contents

vi   *Contents*

Figures

Foreword

Responsible reporting

A few years ago, Peter Morris spoke of the "truth" of project management and the role of scholars in capturing it – specifically to "uncover, evaluate and communicate these truths" (Morris, 2016). I can't imagine many distinctions between the role of scholars and practicing project managers in carrying out these tasks, but Peter did mention one. In comparing social sciences to natural sciences, he said that "truth is not independent of our values" in the former as it is in the latter. And while the traditional values of projects have included their satisfaction of time, scope, and quality measures, the time has come to consider new values – human values – as measures of project success. Achieving these values is dependent on good reporting, making the value of *this* book even higher. And, through this perspective, I'd like to touch on each main section of the book.

Stakeholders have always gone beyond the immediate and usual group of project team members, sponsors, and clients. Most of the time they are not directly known by the project manager as they are two or more steps beyond final project delivery. But in this age of new project truths and increasing public challenges, those who are unknown should be among the first thought of to benefit from our project and management choices.

Data – it is the currency of project reporting. In communicating the work of humanitarian projects, where and how can that currency be spent across the project lifecycles? How will the traditional or typical data sources of spreadsheets, ERPs, and project management systems accommodate new data sources in a future of big data, predictive analytics, and increased privacy regulations? We must be proactive and vigilant, balancing the needs of the project against the individuals involved.

There are so many stories within any given project – why do we remain fixated on the scope, objectives, and deliverables? One of the great values of this book is it reminds us that the basics of good storytelling – language, format, message timing, and visuals – are essential to telling project stories. Exploring creativity in the *reporting process* could allow us to move beyond the typical (but essential) project reporting to tell new stories.

The necessity of *project reports* is, arguably, only exceeded by the creativity in which those needs are satisfied. The visual aids identified in this volume are especially exciting when one thinks of (some of) their eventual rendering along three dimensions. Imagine the possibilities for more informed stakeholder involvement when multi-dimensional information graphics are used to report the metrics of a project's status. (Perhaps a spoiler for Alexia's next book?) The enabling of enhanced decision-making is undeniable.

Any number of *challenges* could affect project reporting, starting with (in this book) systems integration, accuracy, timeliness, and accountability. But what about the challenges that project reporting is trying to affect? The United Nations Sustainable Development Goals are the most notable and in need of greater attention by project managers and project management researchers. It's also equally clear that through the increased sophistication and reliability of project reporting, we stand a greater chance of meeting them.

Writing this foreword hasn't been easy for me, and I'm not entirely sure why. Perhaps the importance of readers seeing these words (the first!) of this book weighed heavily on me. Perhaps it was the need to ensure that reporting is seen as a function that now takes on a measure of moral accountability in "responsible project management." Perhaps I simply didn't want to disappoint my friend and colleague. Perhaps all three?

To overcome this hesitation, I was given the advice to be heartfelt and convincing of the necessity of this book. I've tried to do both. But if there's any doubt, let me be clear. Quite simply, with the unprecedented and challenging public priorities affecting humanity, project managers reporting on the impact of their decisions and their projects couldn't be more essential. And that's the truth.

Beverly Pasian
Utrecht, Netherlands
July 2019

Reference

Morris, P.W.G. (2016). Reflections. *International Journal of Project Management*, 34(2), 365–370. Available at: https://doi.org/10.1016/j.ijproman.2015.08.001.

Acknowledgments

I would like to express sincere appreciation to all the friends and colleagues who provided advice and assistance, especially those who volunteered to critique (Alecia, Anthony, Diane, Jessica, and Mairead) and contribute (Beverly, Louise, and Naomi). Hat tip to Mark, Stefan, Sergio, and Dan. Special thanks to Jonathan Norman for seeing a diamond in the rough, the graphics providers (Hexagon AB, e-Builder (A Trimble Company), Cost Engineering Consultancy, and InEight Inc.) for their generosity, and Routledge for their unflagging patience.

Acronyms and abbreviations

3-D	three-dimensional
4-D	four-dimensional
AI	artificial intelligence
APS	advanced planning and scheduling
BIM	building information modeling
CAD	computer-aided design
CBS	cost breakdown structure
CEO	chief executive officer
CFO	chief financial officer
CIO	chief information officer
COO	chief of operations
CPI	cost performance index
CSF	critical success factors
DMAIC	define, measure, analyze, improve, and control
EAC	estimate at completion
ERP	enterprise resource planning
ETC	estimate to complete
EV	earned value
FF&E	furniture, fixtures, and equipment
GIS	geographic information system
IDE	integrated development environment
IoT	internet of things
IT	information technology
IV&V	independent verification and validation
KPI	key performance indicators
OBS	organizational breakdown structure
OGS	office of general counsel
PM	project manager
PMO	project management office
PPE	personal protective equipment

QA/QC	quality assurance/quality control
RFI	request for information
SME	subject matter expert
SOV	schedule of values
SPI	schedule performance index
WBS	work breakdown structure
WIP	work in progress

1 Introduction

The world is complicated, and messy, with lots of moving pieces. This is true both on a grand scale (the universe, the earth), and on smaller scales (daily life, countries, industries, projects). One way to make sense of the world and its many pieces is by categorizing elements, putting related parts together in such a way that they comprise a whole but can also be analyzed in smaller, more manageable portions. Processes that can be measured and understood can then be controlled. That whole and its parts may be quantified, or may be merely described, or may be analyzed using a mix of the two approaches. The output of such analysis for business purposes is usually a report, a graphic and narrative creation that takes the many (sometimes seemingly disparate) fragments of data and simplifies them into a comprehensible snapshot.

The primary function of reporting is communication. Reports are used to inform stakeholders of status, disseminate information, provide data and news for assimilation and decision-making, and elevate the visibility of problems and opportunities. Reporting also cultivates trust by enabling transparency, encouraging accountability, and celebrating success. The report itself is naturally less important than the decisions that form project outcomes, but it is undoubtedly an indispensable vehicle for such decision-making and contributes to the project permanent record.

There are many different formats for reports, and countless ways of combining information. How does the project team decide which format to use, and what information to include? In the sphere of projects, they make that choice by looking to the project stakeholders. Stakeholders are impacted by projects (and vice versa), but they might not necessarily be an active part of the project universe. As such, they often rely heavily on reporting from the project team in order to make decisions. A tendency to overgeneralize project reports may fool stakeholders into believing they fully comprehend the project status quo. Different stakeholders have different information needs, perspectives, and objectives, and thus they have different expectations of reports, while at the same time wanting the unadulterated facts.

The purpose of this book is to discuss the content and format of project reports, and provide guidelines in the context of available technology, stakeholder and management needs, and obstacles to reporting. The book opens by describing the need for project reports, the stakeholders for which they are produced, and situations in which they may be contractually required. Data, data sources, and data management infrastructure are discussed next, in the context of the project lifecycle. The reader is then engaged with a more in-depth discourse about different types of reports and graphics used in projects, including their audience and timing, with examples, explaining specifically why the report types differ and how they are used. Specifically excluded are typical governance documents used to manage the project on a daily basis, such as checklists, meeting minutes, and forms. The author describes some challenges experienced with project reporting, offering advice on how to avoid some of those challenges and how to approach special-purpose reports. The book concludes with some thoughts on the future of project reporting.

2 Stakeholders

Just as beauty is said to be in the eye of the beholder, the same is true for success. Different stakeholders have different definitions of success. Because stakeholders each have their own motives and perspectives, these definitions of success can be widely divergent, such that a project can conceivably be considered both a success and a failure at the same time. It seems impossible, even ridiculous, but it is true. While cost, schedule, and quality are common measures of success for projects, some stakeholders may judge the success of a project by other measures, such as degree of acceptance, level of prestige, the way the project reflects on them, and much more. Understanding stakeholders is, thus, the key to benefits realization. Chapter 2 – Stakeholders, describes some categories of people who define and can directly or indirectly influence project success.

Assurance

Simply put, decision-making requires information. That information includes data that is correct, timely, complete, unbiased, and reliable. The data can be assembled in seemingly endless combinations, yet must be presented in a usable format for a particular purpose. Reports should be tailored to their intended audience, so as to be concise, comprehensible, consistent, and provide the information needed for stakeholders to stay informed, make decisions, and take action. However, the reporting function must also be dynamic, able to respond to changing project conditions. Decision-making in projects requires accurate, timely, and relevant status reporting, yet all too often reports do not serve their intended purpose. Stakeholders seek the information they need, with a caveat: they also want assurance.

There are several applications of "assurance" as a noun; two of them apply here.[1] One is a state of certainty or confidence in something. The other is a statement intended to provide such confidence. Stakeholders wish to have confidence that the information they receive is accurate and appropriate for their purposes; both internal team members and external consultants provide stakeholders with those assurances. The concept of assurance is closely tied to that of accountability, whereby the project team or consultants providing the data are responsible for the quality, accuracy, appropriateness, and timeliness of the information provided. The importance of such accountability cannot be overstated, as errors need to be corrected immediately lest major decisions be based on the incorrect information and advice given.

Assurance and accountability both assume reporting is unbiased and objective, conditions which (sadly) might not always be true if the report comes from within the project management office (PMO). Independence of external consultants suggests disassociation from the situation and immunity to influence, whereas project team members are often deeply embedded in the culture of the project organization and the tangled relationships therein. Then again, external consultants might not have access to all available data and discussions, and thus might not understand the full picture. If employed as consultants internal to the team, project team members may have dual loyalties – to their employer and to the external client. Such circumstances may make certain responsibilities difficult, such as: critical questioning, impartial status assessment, and delivery of bad news.

Optimism and cognitive delusion are common occurrences when reporting project status; failures tend to be downplayed, and results spun into hopeful forecasts. Delayed reporting of data may result from internal sensitivity, pressure, or politics. All these acts of self-protection can result in an overly positive representation of project performance, blurring risks and change, which then obstructs early action to remedy identified issues.

Stakeholder categories

Before discussing stakeholder expectations, the project team first needs to identify and understand who the project stakeholders are, how much they can impact the project, and how they judge project success. Stakeholders may be individuals, formal groups, and entities such as companies and governments. They each have different levels of motivation, interest, power, and influence, which may change throughout the project.

Responsibilities to project stakeholders may fall into several categories:[2]

- Fiduciary duty
- Decision-making (corporate governance)

- Participation
- Fairness
- Cooperation
- Accountability
- Strategic management
- Legitimization
- Risk management (deflecting criticism)
- Social construction (image)

The number of project stakeholders can be considerable, and failure to address their needs may mean failure of the project. Their connection to the project may be contractual, societal, financial, familial, political, emotional, and more. They may be internal or external to the project, explicit or implicit, and involved at any or every phase of the project lifecycle. The stakeholders list may include: companies, corporate employees, contractors, suppliers, consultants, neighbors, investors, partners, end-users, the media, public officials, public or private agencies, the general public, special interest groups, and even past and future generations.

The mindmap below illustrates just some of the categories of stakeholders that can be found on a project.

For the purposes of reporting, identifying stakeholders also means knowing their role on and connection to the project. From there, their level of involvement, primary concerns, definition of success, language and terminology, and level of tolerance for risk and change can be used to customize and shape reports for them. Stakeholder identification should be revisited periodically during a project, because stakeholders often depart in the middle of the project and new stakeholders arrive.

Communication with stakeholders is one mechanism for establishing and managing their expectations. The recommended stakeholder audience for specific types of reports is provided later in this book.

Internal stakeholders

Governing boards

Some formal oversight bodies on a project and within an organization are stakeholders that serve as a governance mechanism. Examples of these are: board of directors, steering committee, citizen oversight committee, governance, project sponsor, project executive, and audit committee. These groups may enact corporate, legislative, or regulatory-required guardianship of the project, monitoring project progress and providing guidance to project management and leadership. Each has an agreed-upon

Figure 2.1 Stakeholder mindmap.

Source: Nalewaik, Alexia and Mills, Anthony (2016). *Project Performance Review: Capturing the Value of Audit, Oversight, and Compliance for Project Success*, p. 52. London: Routledge.

high level of authority, area of responsibility, and organizational charter. Members of such oversight bodies need to understand the strategic implications, risk, and potential outcomes of project actions; without adequate reporting, they may make decisions based on out-of-context information. The project team may need approvals from governing boards for certain project actions, especially budget approval and changes in goals or scope. A governing board may use its influence and authority to assist the project, solve problems, and resolve issues. Governing boards often serve as an intermediary for reporting to organizational executive officers such as the Chief Executive Officer (CEO), Chief Information Officer (CIO), Chief of Operations (COO), Chief Financial Officer (CFO), and external authorities.

Project or program sponsor

The sponsor is the ultimate executive on the project or program team, a member of the client organization external to the project or program. They approve major project or program activities, changes, and expenditures, monitor the effectiveness of project or program management, and are tasked with both project visioning and removing roadblocks to project or program success. They have authority to direct all staff, secure resources, resolve conflicts, and have sufficient influence to engage with key stakeholders. They may chair the steering committee or other governing boards. The project or program sponsor may serve as an intermediary both within the organization and with external stakeholders.

Chief financial officer (CFO)

The chief financial officer exists at a corporate executive level, often removed from projects yet connected via the monitoring and provision of project financing and governance. The language they use is very specific, and must be understood by the project team. Return on investment (ROI), depreciation of assets, taxation, the time value of money, revenue, color of money (use of funds received from different sources), and expenditures are terminology they use. In the finance office, success of a project may be defined purely on financial metrics. The project team may require approvals and signatures from the CFO for project finance actions. Further, the CFO or treasurer may be a financial delegate or an intermediary for reporting to external funding sources, investors, donors, and shareholders.

Chief information officer (CIO)

The chief information officer exists at a corporate executive level, often removed from projects yet connected via the monitoring and provision of corporate information systems. The CIO will likely be the project sponsor for information technology projects. The language used by the CIO is also very specific, and must be understood by the project team. The project team may require approvals from the CIO for information security and systems-related project resources, activities, and integration.

Program manager

When an organization has several projects all directed toward a certain corporate objective, those projects grouped together are called a program; the entirety of projects within the organization is called a portfolio. The program manager has overall responsibility and accountability for program success, and may report to the program sponsor, governing boards, and/or other corporate executives. They will typically chair program meetings, and have approval authority for program-level actions. Program management may be an intermediary for reporting to program-specific steering committees.

Project manager (PM)

The project manager is internal to the project organization, and has overall responsibility and accountability for project success, reporting to some combination of the program manager, project/program sponsor, governing boards, and/or other corporate executives. They will typically chair project-level meetings, and have approval authority for project actions. Project management may be an intermediary for reporting to project-specific steering committees.

Project or program management office (PMO)

If a project management office is created for the project or program, within the PMO will be found additional leaders, project and program team members, subject matter experts, and contributors. Those leaders may have responsibility for, and oversight of, engineering, design, construction, research, implementation, project controls, document control, procurement, technical support, and more. These project team members may include various team or department leads, who are responsible for direction to departmental or sub-team members, deliverables, meetings, etc.

The PMO typically serves both a project (or program) management and an administrative role on the project, satisfying all required functions for the project (or program) to progress. If there is no centralized project or program management function, functional managers (such as engineering or manufacturing) and functional team members may assume the roles described above in addition to their regular responsibilities.

Office of general counsel (OGC)

The legal office or OGC is a corporate executive group external to the operation of the project, led by chief or general counsel, which is in charge of all legal affairs for the organization. The chief counsel may be an intermediary for reporting to the general public, external regulatory agencies, and special interest groups. The OGC may also manage a whistleblower hotline, oversee an inspector general's office, and be an intermediary for selecting and managing external counsel (lawyers) and advisors. Members of the OGC will typically be involved in the project or program on contractual matters and claims.

Risk officer

The corporate risk officer is part of the corporate executive organization, external to the operation of the project, who is responsible for enterprise risk management, including risk awareness within the organization. This includes current and future risks. They may address market risk, credit risk, and operational risk. The corporate risk officer is likely an intermediary for selecting and managing insurers, reporting to insurers, and ensuring that insurance requirements on the project or program are satisfied.

Other internal stakeholders

Within the owner and project organizations, there are other internal stakeholders and customers who either want or need to be updated on the project. This includes company or project departments (such as human resources, marketing, internal audit, security, and environmental health and safety), cross-cutting functions, teams (such as development, real estate, facilities, procurement, quality, information technology, testing, and operations), and individual employees. These may be direct or indirect stakeholders who are part of the project, champions and thought leaders, subject matter experts (SMEs), contributors, data holders, or people or departments who will be end-users of the project output. Each of these internal stakeholders will need to be identified by the project team.

External stakeholders

Regulatory, licensing, and government agencies

Some organizations, and their projects, are subject to some level of oversight by external agencies. For example, projects that receive public or special-purpose funding will need to satisfy certain requirements and report back to regulatory and government agencies regarding the use, and timing of use, of those funds. Similarly, projects that are created in heavily regulated environments will need to satisfy certain requirements and report back to regulatory and government agencies regarding those requirements. Safety, quality, and environmental restrictions are typical examples. The project sponsor, COO, CFO, or other executive may be the liaison to such agencies, and may approve reports prior to issuance to such agencies.

Financiers

Funding providers are external to the project. They will have certain requirements, restrictions, and strict rules regarding the use of funds, and often require specific reporting. The project sponsor, CFO, or other executive may be the liaison to financiers, and may approve reports prior to issuance to financiers.

Insurers

Insurance providers are external to the project, and provide necessary services to the project. They will have certain requirements, restrictions, and strict rules regarding access to insurance, and often require specific reporting. The project sponsor, chief risk officer, or other executive may be the liaison to insurers, and may approve reports prior to issuance to insurers.

Contractors, consultants, vendors, and suppliers

During the project, the team will usually engage with various external companies to provide goods and services to the project that are necessary for the project's success. Establishing expectations and managing these relationships is part of project management's responsibility, and communication is a two-way process.

In addition to the goods and services provided, the project team will often rely on information and reporting from the external companies, as part of the project reporting process. As with internal documentation and data, the information received from these external providers also needs to be correct, timely, complete, and reliable. While trust may be regarded as a virtue, in the context of a project it can also be dangerous if trust is misplaced. The concept of assurance applies here; trust needs to be periodically justified. Certainty of confidence in data provided by external parties is necessary. As with the goods and services provided, information from external providers may need to be periodically audited for accuracy.

Once the project is completed, depending on the type of project, additional goods and services providers may become clients and customers of the end product. These providers will thus have a vested interest in understanding more about, and monitoring the progress of, the project for their own business purposes.

The general public

The realm of public stakeholders is broad, and includes local communities, potential clients and customers, functional beneficiaries, local businesses, voters and taxpayers, neighbors, potential employees, future generations, and others. These entities can be difficult to understand, and thus unpredictable. Each has different motivations, and different requirements.

Especially for projects intended for end-use by the public, small segments of the population tend to be very passionate and engaged. They may consider themselves to be owners of the end product, or ad hoc overseers, despite a lack of technical knowledge. The general public's expectations of large-scale projects tend to be mismatched with reality, because they do not always understand the complexities and timelines of delivering the project. Lest they become disappointed or belligerent, those expectations, and the accompanying media coverage, need to be managed proactively. The media or communications department or designated liaison may be an intermediary for reporting to public stakeholders, and crafting press releases.

Other external stakeholders

There may be other direct or indirect external stakeholders, with varying levels of legitimacy, who either want or need to be updated on the project. This could include:

- Landowners
- Political beneficiaries (elected officials)
- Activist organizations
- Industry groups (such as lobbyists and professional institutions)
- Unions

- Media
- Groups acting on behalf of the environment
- Former employees
- Volunteers
- Members of a jury
- Other special interest groups
- Other not-for-profit groups

Communication plans should be developed for each of these, as appropriate.

Notes

1 Oxford English Dictionary online. Available at: https://en.oxforddictionaries.com/definition/assurance.
2 Greenwood, Michelle (2007). Stakeholder Engagement: Beyond the Myth of Corporate Responsibility. *Journal of Business Ethics*, 74(4), pp. 315–317. Berlin: Springer.

3   Data

On a typical project, there are large volumes of available data, which must be digested and extracted for decision-making. The larger the project, the more data is produced. Chapter 3 – Data, describes data, data sources, and data management infrastructure in the context of the project lifecycle.

The project lifecycle

How does a project come to be? First it is a concept, then justifications and approvals are necessary before that concept becomes a fully-fledged project based on the needs of the organization. No matter the reasoning used for creating the project, the idea itself is subject to evaluation at some high level of management before it is approved as a project, and again at subsequent decision-making points. Communication and reporting is key to this decision-making process. The management team may be comprised of an executive committee, board of directors, advisory board, or other grouping of decision makers, financiers, and stakeholders. The management team reviewing and providing approvals typically assesses the viability of the idea, may amend the scope of work or approach, makes the go/no-go decision, obtains and approves funding, and then paves the way for that idea to begin becoming a reality. Not every idea will be approved; choices must be made by executives based on priorities, timing, and funding availability. Tangible benefit must be demonstrated in the business case analysis and proposal in order for an idea to be approved. In the typical organization, there may be many projects worthy of action, but only a few will be approved during each planning and budgeting cycle, due to finite availability of funds.

By definition, "a project is a unique, temporary, multidisciplinary, and organised endeavour,"[1] intended to achieve a particular goal, or deliver a particular product or service; the project itself is not the product or service. Projects have a discrete beginning, an end, and any number of steps in the

Figure 3.1 Project lifecycle.

middle. During its lifecycle, a project will naturally progress through various defined phases, and achieve key milestones (important dates or progress points) and objectives. Project phase terminology varies by organization and industry, but can generally be described as initiation, development, execution, and closeout. Some activities defined here in a particular phase may overlap with, or improve upon, deliverables from work undertaken in other project phases.

Figure 3.1 is a timeline that uses project phases as the x-axis, instead of dates.

As the project proceeds through its various phases and achieves key milestones and decision points in its lifecycle, project stakeholders and decision makers seek to receive information that is (specifically for them) meaningful, appropriately actionable, and satisfactorily timely to assist them in making choices and guiding the project. Depending on the organization, project structure, or delivery method, the project phases and activities shown below may be rearranged or may be iterative.

Initiation

When a project is initiated, it is an idea, organizational need, or opportunity that came into existence as a result of deliverables that do not yet exist but are required to satisfy organizational strategic objectives. When the need or opportunity has been refined enough to become the cornerstone of the project concept, it becomes the model against which project success is defined. During the initiation phase, the concept is drafted and refined, along with a first pass at feasibility (technical and economic), and business case (including total cost of ownership, requirements, scope, major resource needs, project justification, preliminary budget, and potential completion date).

The success or failure of a project is often determined during the initiation and development phases. If the cost of the project is understated and the return on investment is overstated, as often occurs in order to obtain project approval, the project will be doomed from the start. During the initiation phase, several projects or viable alternate concepts may be competing against each other for funding, and it is very likely there are not enough funds available to fund all of them. Decisions need to be made using meaningful and reliable information, with documented logical reasoning that identifies clear values and trade-offs. It is very important for the project team to understand that any budget number, no matter how rough, will likely become anchored in stakeholder memory, and will likely be the amount against which final performance is measured, even if significant agreed-upon and approved change has since occurred.

Development

During the development phase, a project execution plan is established for the process of investment of resources required to deliver the project goal. The project plan is essentially a roadmap that should be followed in order for the project to be completed on time and on budget, economically, efficiently, and effectively. The execution strategy relies heavily on input from the project definition, identified constraints, and requirements. Risk assessment and creation of governance is also performed during this phase.

"Governance" is a term used to describe all the processes needed to govern. These processes guide all project management activity, creating constraints, implementing controls, defining interaction, and conferring autonomy and decision-making authority. Governance is the framework within which all project management functions, and is intended to enable accountability, consistency, predictability, and transparency. It affects enterprise management, project management, project controls, procurement, and finance. Sometimes seen as bureaucracy, governance artifacts may include: project charter, contracts, policies and procedures, processes, rules and regulations, workflow, information technology (IT) systems, organizational structure, decision-making processes, communication plans, resource plans, and project documentation.

Key to the development phase is a commitment to action: formal approval for the project start, formation of leadership, and the release of funds and other systems and resources for project use. When the basics of project scope and deliverables have been established, and funds are made available, design/engineering and implementation planning can commence. If development and approval of budgets, cash flow analysis, and confirmation of funding sources was not done during the initiation phase, it will be done now. The development phase will also typically include the creation of scenario-specific estimates and schedules, additional resource requirements, and value engineering with evaluations of different scenarios. Peer reviews and economic analysis will be used to fine-tune development phase deliverables. If product time to market is a priority, this phase will concentrate on streamlining processes, purchasing, and coordination to accelerate the project completion date. Once design and engineering are completed, procurement and contracting decisions will be made, regarding the delivery mechanism that best fits the project.

Execution

Project execution is the longest, most demanding, and most highly dynamic phase of the project lifecycle, during which the highest utilization of resources and activities occurs. The goal of the project execution phase is to create the project deliverables.

During this phase, the project plans, processes, and policies and procedures created during the initiation and development phases are implemented, and project activities and tasks are conducted in accordance with governance, scope, specifications, and requirements. There will be a heavy focus on action, communication, management controls, and monitoring. Areas of emphasis include: procurement, resources, quality, risk, change, testing, and compliance. The bulk of project reporting and information distribution occurs during the execution phase of the project.

Closeout

Closeout is the final phase of the project that often signals a transition to a new lifecycle of maintenance and operations, production, or utilization. During closeout, the project is tested for performance according to specified requirements and acceptance criteria, and then officially delivered. The project ends. The asset or deliverable created by the project then begins the next phase of its life. Formal closeout of the project is necessary for administrative, financial, and legal purposes.

Typical of closeout is the gathering of information and creation of documentation to be used for historic and end-user purposes, future benchmarking, warranties, final accounting (including capitalization and depreciation), commissioning, training, and transition/turnover. Funds, staff, equipment, and other resources are released for other uses. Contracts and purchase orders will be closed, contingency and reserves released, and the project organization itself may be dissolved. Contractors, consultants, vendors, and suppliers may be subject to performance evaluations, and lessons learned recorded. A user satisfaction survey may be conducted either at closeout or some specified period of time after closeout.

Data sources

Many different systems are used to manage a project. These systems both contain and generate project information, in many different formats and configurations. These sources of data, or systems, are important not only at the time of report generation, but also in the event of future claims and litigation, and as historical data. Some of these data sources and systems are identified and described below. Project reports may be generated directly from these systems, but more often combine data from multiple systems with analysis and narrative.

Spreadsheets

Spreadsheets, such as those created and generated in Microsoft Excel, are one of the most commonly used tools to compile and manage project information, and generate reports. This is especially true if existing corporate and project systems do not lend themselves to ease of use, are outdated, cannot interface with other systems, or do not capture the type of information needed by the project team and stakeholders. Data is often exported from existing systems, and manipulated within a spreadsheet to the format and content needed. Spreadsheets can also be used as an intermediary in data transfer, where information is exported from one system into a spreadsheet and then imported from the spreadsheet to a different system. Challenges with the use of spreadsheets include incorrect formulas, missing links, hidden columns and rows, errors in data entry, and the high potential for falsification.

ERP systems

In many companies, stand-alone accounting and financial software has been replaced with modular Enterprise Resource Planning (ERP) systems. These information management software packages integrate many kinds of financial, business intelligence, and operations information in one system, often including inventory, asset, sales, marketing, procurement, and human resources data. Such systems may integrate management processes, such as electronic workflow approvals. A major benefit of these systems is that they serve as a centralized repository of information, reducing the need for entry of data into multiple systems, thus reducing staff level of effort and risk of errors while improving data integrity and retrievability.

There is a tendency for companies with an ERP system to try to use it for managing a project and providing project cost controls. Some ERP systems do have specific add-on modules for project costing, materials planning, and asset management, which can be useful to a certain degree but might not always be as functional as stand-alone project management software. Corporate workflow and approvals are often not the same as project workflow and approvals. Care must be taken with these systems to ensure both the workflow process and cost coding map are correctly transferred to other external systems needed for project management and reporting; a standard chart of accounts will ease the exchange of data between systems. As with other systems used on a project, the database of historical information may be useful.

Finance

Financial activities may be captured within an ERP system, or in a stand-alone accounting system. Accounting systems are intended to capture financial data, enable compliance, and ensure accurate reporting for financial statements. Although financial accounting and project cost management are fundamentally different, they rely on the same or similar information captured in different ways and during different time periods. Financial accounting must satisfy accepted accounting practices and principles, and taxation, regulation, and other legal requirements. Access to financial systems is typically (and should be) limited to authorized finance department staff, which hampers the use of financial systems as project management systems.

A key difference between financial accounting and project cost management (or project controls) is in the packaging and treatment of project and activity cost data. Accounting data is organized in cost centers according to a chart of accounts designed to support company operations, with a focus on accounts payable, accounts receivable, and the general ledger. The chart of accounts may be a cost breakdown structure (CBS) or organizational breakdown structure (OBS). In contrast, project cost management assigns costs to project-specific activities, through a WBS, which are by their very nature more numerous than the chart of accounts.

The figure below depicts a project cost breakdown structure, and associated labor costs.

There are some challenges that may be experienced when using financial systems for project cost information. First, accounting systems may lack the granularity of data and level of detail to adequately produce meaningful

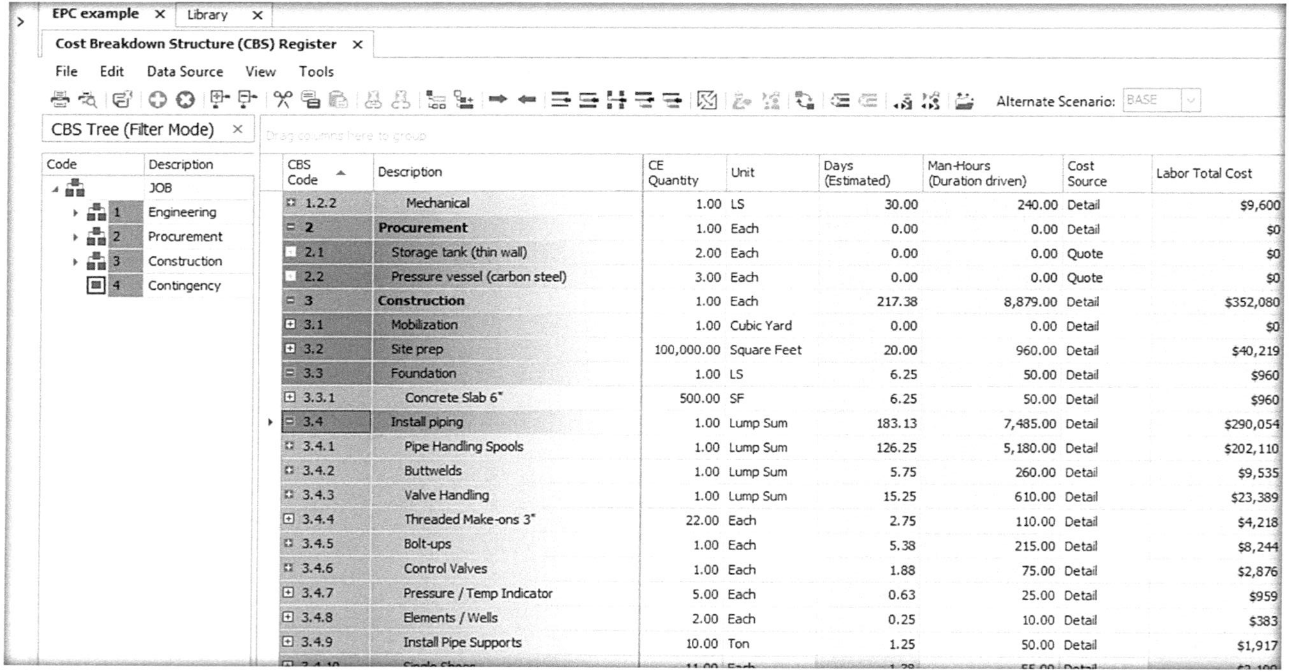

CBS Code	Description	CE Quantity	Unit	Days (Estimated)	Man-Hours (Duration driven)	Cost Source	Labor Total Cost
1.2.2	Mechanical	1.00	LS	30.00	240.00	Detail	$9,600
2	Procurement	1.00	Each	0.00	0.00	Detail	$0
2.1	Storage tank (thin wall)	2.00	Each	0.00	0.00	Quote	$0
2.2	Pressure vessel (carbon steel)	3.00	Each	0.00	0.00	Quote	$0
3	Construction	1.00	Each	217.38	8,879.00	Detail	$352,080
3.1	Mobilization	1.00	Cubic Yard	0.00	0.00	Detail	$0
3.2	Site prep	100,000.00	Square Feet	20.00	960.00	Detail	$40,219
3.3	Foundation	1.00	LS	6.25	50.00	Detail	$960
3.3.1	Concrete Slab 6"	500.00	SF	6.25	50.00	Detail	$960
3.4	Install piping	1.00	Lump Sum	183.13	7,485.00	Detail	$290,054
3.4.1	Pipe Handling Spools	1.00	Lump Sum	126.25	5,180.00	Detail	$202,110
3.4.2	Buttwelds	1.00	Lump Sum	5.75	260.00	Detail	$9,535
3.4.3	Valve Handling	1.00	Lump Sum	15.25	610.00	Detail	$23,389
3.4.4	Threaded Make-ons 3"	22.00	Each	2.75	110.00	Detail	$4,218
3.4.5	Bolt-ups	1.00	Each	5.38	215.00	Detail	$8,244
3.4.6	Control Valves	1.00	Each	1.88	75.00	Detail	$2,876
3.4.7	Pressure / Temp Indicator	5.00	Each	0.63	25.00	Detail	$959
3.4.8	Elements / Wells	2.00	Each	0.25	10.00	Detail	$383
3.4.9	Install Pipe Supports	10.00	Ton	1.25	50.00	Detail	$1,917

Figure 3.2 Project cost breakdown structure.

Source: Graphic provided by InEight, using InEight Basis software.

project reports. Standard reports generated by accounting systems, such as financial statements, summarize operations data but may lack detail on specific projects. The typical accounting system does not contain enough data or sophistication to effectively manage projects. Second, the timeline of the project may span more than one fiscal year; accounting systems are configured to report on a fiscal year or year-to-date basis, and have difficulty managing data that spans several years. Third, financial accounting may be done on a cash or accrual basis, whereas project cost accounting is performed on a cash basis (in which expenditures are recorded during the same time period as when the expense is incurred) but may also include accrued (committed) expenditures for forecasting purposes.

Procurement

Procurement activities may be captured within an ERP system, or in a stand-alone purchasing system. Procurement software is used to record and track purchases made by an organization, such as equipment, material, and services. It may be used for tracking and approving requisitions and purchase orders, renting and leasing, contracting, ordering products or services, inventory management, tracking invoice receipt and payment, managing vendors, and more.

Purchases for a project may be entered into the procurement management system. It is important for the team to know whether these items are also shown in the project management system, to avoid duplication or accidental omission. As with other systems used on a project, the database of historical information may be useful, and a standard chart of accounts will ease the exchange of data between systems. Individual suppliers may have their own chart of accounts, which will need to be mapped to the accounts established in the project systems.

Asset management

Asset management activities may be captured within an ERP system, or in a stand-alone asset management system. Asset management software is used to record and track assets through their lifecycle, from initial procurement to maintenance to disposal. It may be used for capital, hardware, software, digital, and other types of assets. Information captured may include inventory tracking, location, utilization, asset performance, vendor performance, licensing, depreciation and capitalization, shipping and logistics, preventive and predictive maintenance, parts, regulatory compliance, and more.

Purchases for a project (such as furniture, fixtures, and equipment [FF&E]), and end products from a project (such as a building or production line), may also be entered into the asset management system. As with other systems used on a project, the database of historical information may be useful to the organization, and a standard chart of accounts will ease the exchange of data between systems.

Project management systems

Project management software has been developed and evolved specifically to address project-specific processes and activities. Capabilities typically include change management, scheduling, milestone tracking, estimating, resource management, cost and schedule control, project cost accounting, procurement, contract administration, document control, issue tracking, development, testing, historic database, and much more. For project cost accounting, the system enables management of budgets, commitments, and expenditures. Tools may be included in the software capabilities, specifically for stage-gated projects and project phases. Some project management systems are configured as a virtual team meeting room, containing information on the organizational structure, and providing capabilities such as messaging, texting, document markup, polling, task management, process workflow and approvals, calendar and contact sharing, collaboration tools, checklists, and more. Project management software often has built-in reporting and invoicing capabilities.

The project team will create within the project management software a hierarchical framework, a work breakdown structure (WBS) or organizational breakdown structure (OBS), against which all activities and work packages are organized, put in order, and tracked. The structure may be based on a product (deliverable) or process, and provides a common frame of reference for reporting. Activities in both the estimate and schedule are each mapped to a WBS element. If the organization has more than one project, it is advisable for all projects to have the same WBS, enabling consistent categorization of information and comparisons between projects. The objective is to report accuracy, consistency, comparability, and flow of information.

The software may be installed on a computer or other device, or may be web-based, hosted, and maintained by an external provider. Specific elements of project management software are discussed below; these may also be stand-alone software, or spreadsheets. The project may use some but not all of the functionalities and specific types of software shown below. Some of the software types shown below have functions that may overlap with other software packages.

Estimating

Data used in estimating may come from many different sources, including published cost guides and information obtained directly from suppliers. It may be historic data, gathered internally to the organization, which has been escalated and indexed to match the project year and location.

Estimating software is a highly specialized tool that serves the very precise needs of project estimators. Stand-alone estimating software may be more sophisticated than that found in an all-in-one project management system. Estimate documentation and cost particulars are often compiled and kept in an electronic cost-estimating database, within specialty software. The database will be organized according to the project WBS, and will include resource costs of labor, equipment, materials, subcontractors, markups, overhead, taxes, and other costs by category, trade, and region, including historical costs and indices. Additional features and capabilities include assembly costing, quantity take-off, waste percentages for materials, pricing of alternatives, management of allowances, and more. Estimating software often has a built-in reporting function that includes graphics.

Scheduling

Scheduling software packages are a highly specialized tool for sequencing project activities and planning the project. Stand-alone scheduling and project planning software packages, especially those designed for manufacturing and production, may be more sophisticated than that found in an all-in-one project management system. The software may include a database for cost and resource data, and map activities to the project WBS. Schedule management features and capabilities include resource planning, monitoring productivity, tracking variances, managing change and float, earned value, performance measurement, collaboration, cash flow, forecasting, advanced analytics, and capturing data for historical purposes. Advanced planning and scheduling systems (APS) capabilities for manufacturing and production include what-if scenarios, decision-making capabilities, real-time operational visibility, equipment scheduling, optimization, demand planning, and much more. Scheduling software often has a built-in reporting function that includes graphics.

Cost management

Cost management software applications are not necessarily the same as those used for estimating. Cost management is concerned with what specific items and/or activities should cost and what they actually cost, mapped to the project total budget and WBS line items. Project cost management and project cost accounting are not quite the same as financial accounting; the scope is much more complete. Cost management features and capabilities include budgeting, estimating, resource planning, monitoring cost and productivity, tracking variances, managing change and contingency, collaboration, earned value, performance measurement, forecasting, advanced analytics, and capturing data for historical purposes. Cost management software often has a built-in reporting function that includes graphics.

Contract management

Contract management is part of the procurement cycle. The function includes administration and management of contracts and change, tracking of invoice and payment, evaluation of performance, benchmarking, and tracking of commitments. On a project, contract management software and purchasing software may be separate, especially where contract management is project-specific and procurement is an organizational department that manages entity-wide purchasing. Stand-alone contract management software may be more sophisticated than that found in an all-in-one project management system. Additional features and capabilities may include hierarchical approval workflows based on quantitative monetary thresholds, a library of standardized contract clauses, complex counterparty relationships, contract lifecycle management, collaboration, compliance monitoring, and more. Contract management software often has a built-in reporting function that includes graphics.

Purchasing

Purchasing software can be used to record and track purchases made for the project (including labor, materials, equipment, and other resources), and keep track of vendors and contractors. Capabilities typically include tracking of requisitions and purchase orders, receipt of goods or services, inventory, invoice and payment data, and a supplier database. Purchasing is a part of the procurement cycle. The software may also include procurement functions, such as the process of sourcing and selecting vendors, negotiating contracts, supplier audits, electronic catalogs, supplier relationships management, and conducting quality evaluations.

Purchasing functions within the project management system will be very similar to those in an ERP system, or in a stand-alone purchasing system, except they will be project-specific instead of organization-specific. As mentioned previously, it is important for the team to distinguish between project and organizational purchasing systems, to avoid duplication or accidental omission when reporting expenditures. Purchasing software often has a built-in reporting function that includes graphics.

Risk management

Project risk management software is another highly specialized tool that addresses not just the identification and management of project risks but also their potential impact on project cost, schedule, and quality. Stand-alone risk management software may be more sophisticated than that found in an all-in-one project management system. The software typically enables risk register creation and management, quantification, issue management, and mitigation plans. The software often includes impact and probability analysis and may include Monte Carlo-type risk modeling, used to calculate monetary contingency and recommended schedule float for various probabilities. Research in risk management is yielding new types of software that incorporate predictive analytics and artificial intelligence in cost and schedule risk models. Risk management software often has a built-in reporting function that includes sophisticated graphics.

Document control

The document control system is the primary repository of all official project documentation, often in conjunction with a physical and/or additional digital storage facility. In addition to contract files (including technical documents appended to the contract, and change orders), the project charter, governance processes (such as policies and procedures, and the project management plan), and supporting documentation for schedules and estimates, document control will capture any necessary documentation for both historic and legal records. These may include correspondence, meeting minutes, lessons learned, activity logs, photographic records, and various other forms, checklists, and reports. Document control systems have additional capabilities in collaboration, version control, access control for data security, audit trails, regulatory compliance, indexing, and classification.

Other systems

In addition to the systems mentioned above, other systems accessed by the project team will typically depend on the industry served by the project, the project management methodology used, and the delivery method.

- Software used for major events and administrative projects may include mobile project management applications (apps) and decision tools.
- Manufacturing projects may require specialty manufacturing PM software, production management tools, supply chain management, optimization capabilities, and quality/six-sigma management tools.
- Construction software might include building information modeling (BIM), geospatial data in geographic information systems (GIS), software specific to construction drawings, incident reporting systems, claims management systems, and mobile applications (apps) for data collection.
- Design and engineering projects will utilize computer-aided design (CAD) and drafting software, collaborative document annotation/concurrent design software, simulation and modeling tools, and highly specialized engineering and computational systems.
- Software development and information technology projects might utilize programming tools, business process and data modeling systems, an integrated development environment (IDE), quality control, and risk management tools to address information security vulnerabilities.
- New product development may use digital prototyping software, 3-D printing, business intelligence reporting, compliance management tools, project prioritization tools.
- Research projects may require data management, specialized engineering and computational systems, funding source management, data modeling systems, and tools for lessons learned and compliance.

These are just some of the systems used in project management that contribute data and information to the project reporting process. It is important to understand which systems are available, and decide which are necessary and helpful in project reporting.

Note

1 International Project Management Association (2015). *Individual Competence Baseline®, version 4.0.* The Netherlands: IPMA.

4 The reporting process

For stakeholders, their biggest challenge for decision-making is knowing where to get the right information. This often requires time and reliance on others. The majority of conventional database systems generate reports that focus on the immediate present or recent past, meaning what has happened up to and including a particular point in time, known as a data date. Such systems also enable management by exception, wherein crisis and outlier information is provided to the appropriate stakeholder for immediate consideration. Chapter 4 – The Reporting Process, describes the format, language, and timing of reports, and different types of visuals that can be used to help tell the project story.

Format

Project communications plan

Project reporting is done at many different hierarchical levels, including: enterprise, departmental, team, task, and individual. When developing a project communications plan, the project team identifies the information needs of stakeholders and stakeholder categories, and then determines how and when that information will be collected and communicated. For each report, the format, timing, distribution method, storage/disposition, and audience should be established. Distribution methods include face-to-face meetings and calls, written reports, publicly posted reports, social media, email, messaging, and virtual systems/online meeting rooms.

Communication with stakeholders is a two-way street that requires a certain amount of outreach and input. Activities formulated to engage with stakeholders and receive information from them include town hall meetings, polls, project website, blog, and social media.

Report format

Accept this truth now or suffer the consequences – there is no one-size-fits-all report. Many have tried and failed to create one, or developed one that was ineffective and did not serve its purpose(s). When developing a report format, the project team needs to consider the unique report audience, the intent and uses of the report, the level of confidentiality, and the decisions that will be made based on the report. Given these four variables, it is especially difficult to find a single all-purpose user-friendly report format that is able to adequately communicate complex project information to multiple types of stakeholders at multiple levels of management.

The level of report detail, frequency, and timing needs to be correlated directly with the stakeholder proximity to the project. Reports must ensure stakeholder understanding, quality, appropriate content, confidentiality, and clarity in order to communicate adequately and appropriately, and enable decision-making.

Key to creating a fitting report are the following concepts:

- Stakeholder role
- Primary concerns
- Level of comprehension
- Definition of success
- Managing expectations
- Level of tolerance for risk and change
- Decisions to be made by the stakeholder
- Level of involvement
- Data sources for the report
- Frequency of reporting
- Periodic vs. situational reporting
- Confidentiality requirements
- Public disclosure requirements

Certain organization departments may already have standardized reports that serve their internal and/or external purposes. If the report to be used or developed is one that will be issued periodically or will be used as a format for all projects, consistent structure is especially important, so as to avoid confusion in reading the report from period to period, and project to project. Report formats and examples for various types of reports are provided later in this chapter.

Language

Project reports are part of the permanent project record. In general, formality of language is recommended for project reports, especially those sent to external stakeholders. Not only does this ensure the report content is businesslike and professional, it also avoids potential complications should the project documentation be needed for legal purposes. The same is true for content – reports should generally be contained to complete and accurate facts, not opinions. Proofreading and quality control are essential; grammar and spelling need to be correct, and report authors should have some skill in business writing. Reports should avoid jargons and acronyms. Some schools of thought believe all project reports should be written in the past tense, as the observations have already occurred at the time of report writing.

Stakeholders are a product of their unique background, education, experiences, and environment, and use certain language as a result. Perhaps the most important part of understanding stakeholders is insight into how much they really comprehend the project, and their capacity to communicate in shared project language and terminology. They are not necessarily in the same type of business as the owner organization that has commissioned the project. Project stakeholders do not always have the same command and level of involvement as project team members, and their needs are quite different from those of people who are very close to the project. If stakeholders lack comprehension of technical concepts, their needs will not be served, they might not be able to make a decision, they can accidently misuse the data, and the project may even be inadvertently designed to the wrong requirements. Stakeholders may even need particular information in order to make decisions, but lack the language to use when asking for it, or might not even know it exists. Often, stakeholders need to be trained and periodically re-trained in the language used for project reports; they need to be taught data literacy, and need to be frequently reminded of project concepts, processes, and history. Many stakeholders, especially those on advisory boards and citizen's oversight committees, cannot visualize the final product when looking at engineering drawings and schematics; these stakeholders require 3-D renderings and/or 4-D models (either physical or virtual) to fully understand the project. Such situations, and many others, mean the message and reporting need to be specifically tailored to the audience.

Level of detail

A common complaint from project executives is that they are inundated with large quantities of irrelevant information, while they are simultaneously somehow unable to obtain the information they really need. In this situation, the reporting and communication are data-rich, but information-poor. If information is too burdensome, stakeholders may become overwhelmed by information overload, confusing the recipient of the report, and effectively burying risk and key information in the details. On the other hand, if there is insufficient information in the report, risk will again be hidden, and decisions might be made on guesses or assumptions in lieu of data. There needs to be just enough information in the report to tell the story at a glance, without confusion.

Timing

Many project reports are periodic, meaning they are prepared and presented on a regular basis. That basis is typically monthly, bi-weekly, or weekly, although it may be as frequent as daily. Exceptions to this are reports that are required by the contract or delivery method, which will have specific due dates and may be tied to project milestones or stage gates, and payment. Other specialized reports may be prepared on an as-needed basis, instead of a periodic basis. Recommended timing for each type of report is provided later in this chapter.

Note that some reports require more time to prepare than others, and real-time updating might not always be possible (depending on the systems and data sources contributing to the report). The time and resources needed to assemble the report need to be considered when establishing the timing for recurring reporting.

Executive summary

Any project report longer than two pages (excluding the cover page) should contain an executive summary. An executive summary is an introductory section of the report, usually just a couple of paragraphs, that encapsulates the most pertinent facts and action items from the body of the report.[1] It also sets the overall tone for the report, serves to manage expectations, and directs stakeholder attention to the most pertinent findings or issues.

Document storage

Project reports form an important body of knowledge regarding project history, and a paper trail. Hardcopies of reports, and locked electronic formats (such as pdfs) are the easiest way to prevent report alteration and secure the information contained within for legal and historic purposes. Report originals, or electronic files, need to be stored properly in a centralized physical or electronic location. They should be easy to retrieve. The organization may have very specific requirements regarding document storage, archiving, and disposal.

Contact details

Certain types of reports should contain contact information, in case the report audience needs to discuss the report or obtain more detail. For public-facing reports, the contact information should be for appointed public-facing project team members, such as the media liaison, or a general email inbox that is established specifically for the project and checked periodically.

Visuals

Reports benefit considerably from the addition of visual images, which help to present complex material, numeric data, and narratives in a simpler, graphic manner, or supplement written descriptions. Many types of project management systems and software have the ability to generate graphics for reports. In addition to systems specific to project management, there are websites and apps that are specifically designed to generate graphics and enable visual communication. Spreadsheet, word processing, and presentation/slide creation software packages also have embedded graphics tools, and can import data from more sophisticated statistical analysis software.

It is important to note that, just as visuals can help describe projects, they can also detract. Too many visuals can make a project report appear cluttered, and distract from key information. Some graphics can be difficult to understand; visual information needs to be carefully tailored to its intended audience, and described. Color can be used to enhance reports, but too many colors can confuse. Clutter and readability are common issues when project reports are viewed on mobile devices, due to screen size.

Different types of graphics and visual aides are described below.

Map and map chart

For projects with a geographic element, maps are a useful visual to include in a project report. To make the map even more valuable, various types of layers can be added (such as dot distribution or dot density) and the map can be formatted with color-coding (known as a choropleth map, shown below), markers, and a legend.

The map chart shown in Figure 4.1 displays the number of users of a product, per country. The darker the color shown, the more users there are in that location.

Figure 4.1 Map chart example.

Less common are non-geographic map charts. Cartograms are a special kind of map chart, which distort or exaggerate map boundaries to convey information. Map charts may use clusters of shapes instead of traditional map boundaries.

Photograph

Photographs are often included in a detailed project status report, daily reports, and testing and inspection reports. They are used to demonstrate progress, goods received, quality issues, weather conditions, and more. Photographs are an important part of the project historic record, and provide critical pieces of evidence in claims and legal proceedings.

Simple text

As appealing as complicated and colorful visuals may be, simple text is also an option when showing data. Graphics can actually under-emphasize data, whereas the use of varying sizes of text and color can be used to accentuate information and draw the reader's attention to certain statistics.

95% of project risks have been eliminated

Figure 4.2 Simple text example.

Table

Tables are used to display and sort data that is systematically arranged in relational rows and columns. The data may be qualitative or quantitative. A header row may be added to describe each column by category, and the entire table can be formatted with color, shading, and borders. Values in the table can be encoded with color to create a highlight table. Tables are an often-used communication tool, and can be easier to read than a bullet point list. Data is often pulled from tables to populate charts; if feasible, both the table and chart may be shown in the project report.

In Figure 4.3, a table is used to provide data on project productivity. Each row of the table contains information on items in the project CBS. The columns in the table provide detailed statistics regarding budget, estimate, and productivity in man-hours.

Scatter plot

Scatter plots are used to graph two quantitative variables against two axes, showing a possible correlation (relationship) between the variables. Color-coding can be used to display additional variables. A regression trendline or trendcurve can be added to a scatter plot, representing the "best fit" for the data shown and making the relationship clearer for the audience.

In Figure 4.4, a trendline did not contribute new insight into project variances over time, so it was omitted.

A bubble chart is a special kind of scatter plot that displays three dimensions of data, where the sizes of the bubbles represent the values in the third series of data. Figure 5.21 is an example of a bubble chart.

A bullseye chart is another type of scatter plot that graphs quantitative data against two desired or expected ranges, such as earned value plotted against schedule and cost targets.

Line chart

A line chart is used to show trends in data. Line charts are often used to display changes over time, where the x-axis represents time. The line (or lines, if different data sets are being plotted against the same x-axis) actually connects a series of data points, which may or may not be emphasized in the chart. The line or curve can be smoothed, or added as an overlay that represents a "best fit" to scattered data.

The line chart shown below illustrates cumulative project expenditures per month.

Figure 4.3 Table example.

Source: Graphic provided by InEight, using InEight Basis software.

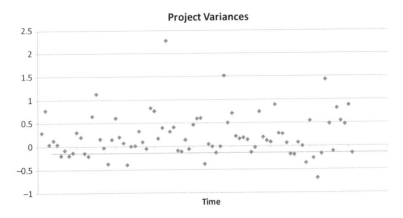

Figure 4.4 Scatter plot example.

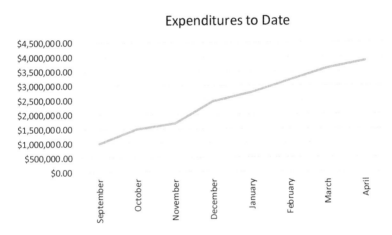

Figure 4.5 Line chart example.

Bar chart/column chart

Bar charts are used to compare values across discrete categories at a single point in time; the bar chart shown below illustrates expenditures for each month. The chart may run vertically, or horizontally, with each category labeled along the axis. A horizontal bar chart is most useful if the text label is long. Categories described in a bar chart are usually qualitative.

The bar chart shown below illustrates project expenditures per month, using the same data as Figure 4.5 – the Line chart example.

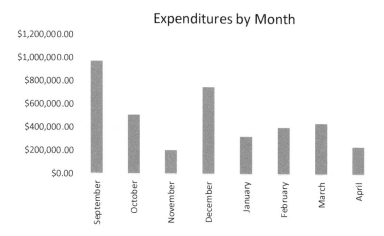

Figure 4.6 Bar chart example.

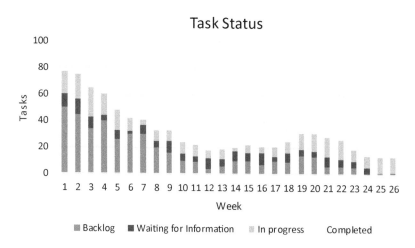

Figure 4.7 Stacked bar chart example.

Clusters of columns or bars may be used to compare changes over time, as can stacked columns or bars. Stacked columns or bars cannot be used for negative values. A trend line or target line can also be added to a bar chart.

The stacked bar chart below shows the number of various tasks by status, and the change per week.

An alternative to a bar chart is a Sankey diagram, which is used to show various data sets broken down into components. A Marimekko chart is a stacked chart that displays a third dimension of data by varying the widths of the columns.

Histogram

A histogram is a specialized chart that displays frequencies within a distribution of quantitative data; the histogram shown below groups stakeholders by age. While it resembles a bar chart, it is not a bar chart because a histogram represents only one variable. A line can also be added to a histogram, representing cumulative values. A project S-curve, described and illustrated later in this book, is essentially a cumulative histogram.

The histogram shown below groups stakeholders by age. The height of each bar describes the number of stakeholders per group.

Pie chart

A pie chart is a circular statistical chart used to graphically represent part-to-whole relationships, or relative contributions to a total; the pie chart shown below groups claims by category. Each pie piece represents the relative contribution of the data, shown as a percentage; each single percentage (1%) equates to an angle of 3.6 degrees on the circle, wherein a full

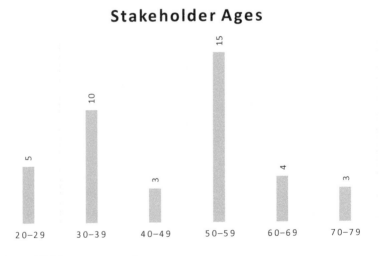

Figure 4.8 Histogram example.

rotation of the circumference of the circle is 360 degrees. A legend may be added around the circumference of the circle, or separately. A pie chart is most useful for a small number of parts (up to five or six), or similarly proportioned parts; adding too much data to a pie chart results in a chart that is cluttered and difficult to read. Pie charts cannot be used for negative values.

The pie chart shown below groups and describes claims according to their status of resolution, and provides statistical data.

There are many different variations on (and terminology for) pie charts, including doughnut charts, multi-level pie charts, polar area diagrams, wedge stack graphs, sunburst charts, waffle charts, and more.

Tree map

Similar to a pie chart, a tree map is used to provide an illustration of the relative size or contribution of different hierarchically structured quantitative data groupings, using nested figures. Data is most often represented as rectangles. A tree map is most useful for a very large number of parts, or imbalanced parts of a whole. Adding color enables the audience to see patterns within the data. Tree maps cannot be used for negative values.

The tree map shown below groups and describes funding amounts by source, and provides statistical data.

A similar type of map, using circles, is called a bubble map.

Number of Claims

Figure 4.9 Pie chart example.

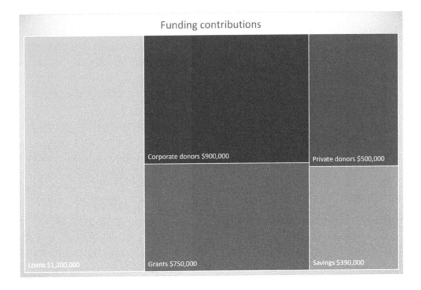

Figure 4.10 Tree map example.

Funding progress

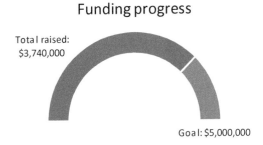

Figure 4.11 Radial gauge example.

Gauge

A radial (speedometer) is used to show quantitative data on a circular or linear scale, most often indicating performance against a target or goal or to represent a percentile measure. A gauge can display only one data set. Shading and/or a pointer are used to represent performance, a target value, or contextual metric.

The gauge shown below graphically describes funds raised to date, compared to the goal, and provides statistical data.

An alternative to a radial gauge is a linear (thermometer) gauge.

Spider chart/radar graph

A spider chart (also known as a radar graph) can be used to display multivariate data against quantitative variables. Each radial line (axis) represents a different category for the subject data, typically labeled at the end point of each axis. It is useful for displaying outliers and similarities.

The spider chart below illustrates the quantity of project risks, grouped by category, and compares the statistical information between two years.

Slope graph

A slope graph is used to map changes in values, or relationships between variables, wherein related variables are connected by a line. It is useful for illustrating changes in data, and comparisons (relative difference) between data sets, and does so more effectively than a bar chart.

The slope graph below describes the quantity of risks, grouped by category, and compares the statistical information between two years. The data used is the same as above, in Figure 4.12 – the Spider chart example.

Flowchart

A flowchart is a diagram that displays a sequence of steps, actions, and/or choices involved in a function, process, workflow, or system. Each step in the flowchart is represented by a shape (such as a box for an activity, a parallelogram for input/output, an oval for a start or end point, and a

Figure 4.12 Spider chart example.

Figure 4.13 Slope graph example.

diamond for a decision point), connected by arrows that illustrate the flow of activity. A flowchart is a graphic representation of a process. In a project report, a flowchart can be used to show steps remaining to be taken, document flow, data flow, system controls, milestones, obstacles (such as approvals or requirements) to be overcome in order to progress, and many other scenarios.

The flowchart below describes the workflow for a stage-gate budgeting process.

Activity diagrams, state diagrams, directed graphs, and Warnier/Orr diagrams are all types of flowcharts.

Mindmap

A mindmap is a way of visually categorizing and structuring thoughts and ideas along branches. It is a diagram for arranging concepts around a central theme. Mindmaps can be useful when showing hierarchical structure, and brainstorming. Another good use of mindmaps is in capturing and conveying lessons learned at the end of the project.

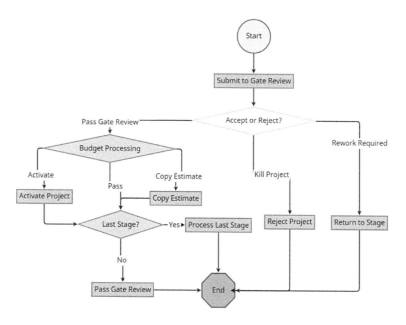

Figure 4.14 Flowchart example.

Source: Graphic provided by Hexagon, using EcoSys software.

The stakeholder graphic in Chapter 2 – Stakeholders, Figure 2.1, is a mindmap of stakeholder categories.

3-D and 4-D graphics

Physical and computerized models of prototypes and final products can be a useful way to communicate spatial design concepts to stakeholders, and to manage the design process. Adding a fourth dimension, time, enables the project team to show how the project evolves along the project time-line, from start to completion.

Note

1 It is sad, but true, that some stakeholders read no more of the report than the executive summary.

5 Types of reports

There is no single correct way to write a project report, because the report itself depends on its audience and the available data. That said, there are some consistent types of reports. Chapter 5 – Types of Reports, goes into greater detail about some different types of reports generated by projects, including their content, use, timing, and intended audience.

The majority of project reports are backward-looking, and are based on the concept of management by exception. This means they have a tendency to focus on situations that deviate from the norm or the plan, and assume the plan was realistic in the first place. Information (data) on that deviation is identified and captured, then provided to the appropriate person for that particular situation, so they can act upon it. Responsibility for creating and distributing reports will depend on the structure of the project management team, knowledge of the project status and issues, and access to data sources.

Dashboard reports

A project dashboard report is intended to communicate large quantities of comprehensive project information in a compact (often one-page) format. It tends to rely upon graphics and color to convey complicated information. A dashboard may use a stoplight-style graphic, to highlight serious issues (red), potential challenges (yellow), and activities that are going according to plan (green). Production of a dashboard report, more than other reports, relies on data gathered from many sources. Dashboard reports are useful for project monitoring and reporting the project status at that moment.

The dashboard report shown below for a single project includes the at-a-glance status of schedule and cost, using a radial gauge to display the schedule performance index (SPI) and cost performance index (CPI). It

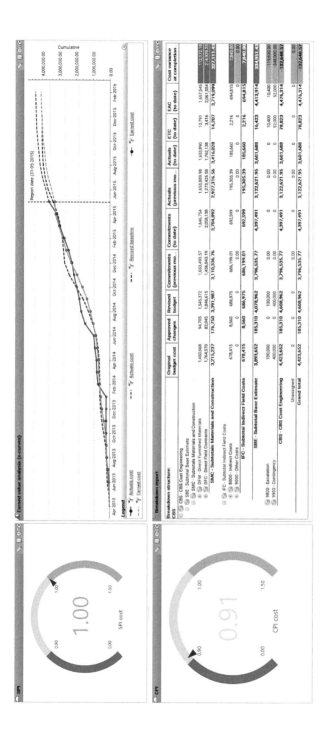

Figure 5.1 Dashboard report example.

Source: Graphic provided by Cost Engineering Consultancy, using Cleopatra Enterprise software.

uses S-curves to describe cost performance per month as part of earned value analysis (with the data date indicated by a vertical line), and uses a table to provide actual cost, commitment, and forecast data organized according to the project cost breakdown structure (CBS). An SPI of greater than one (positive) indicates more work was accomplished than was planned. A CPI of less than one (negative) indicates cost performance is below that planned.

However, there is no one way to develop and present a dashboard report; the content and graphics will vary depending on the intent of the report and available data.

The dashboard report shown below for a portfolio of projects depicts the budgeted and forecasted costs per project, and percent complete. In addition to numeric data in a table, risk data (issues) by type and project are represented graphically and simple text calls attention to change, safety, and quality statistics.

And, giving one more example of the diversity that can be found in dashboard reports, the dashboard report shown below for a portfolio of projects includes a list of projects and each project's current budget. A pie

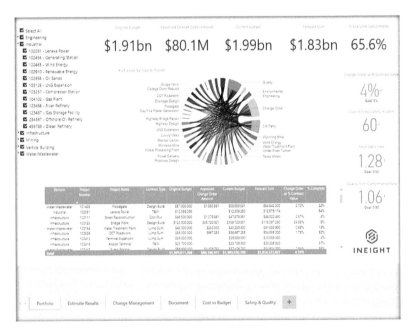

Figure 5.2 Dashboard report example #2.

Source: Graphic provided by InEight using InEight Basis software.

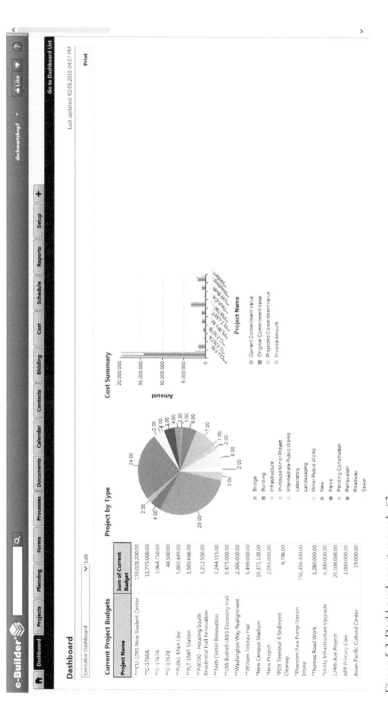

Figure 5.3 Dashboard report example #3.

Source: Graphic provided by e-Builder (A Trimble Company), using e-Builder Enterprise software.

chart is used to display the concentration of projects by type, and a bar chart describes the current, original, projected, and invoiced amounts per project.

A visual history report is a specific type of dashboard for kanban projects.

A dashboard report is often issued on an annual and monthly basis, but may also be produced on-demand for specific meetings. Stakeholders interested in a dashboard report may include, but are not limited to, governing boards, the project or program sponsor, project and organizational executives, and financiers.

A3 report

Named for the 11×17 size of paper often used for this one-page report, the A3 dashboard report is a highly condensed report that uses visual means to communicate process problems on lean six sigma projects. The report format itself mirrors the DMAIC cycle (define, measure, analyze, improve, and control), also known as a PDCA (plan, do, check, act) cycle or Deming cycle, in a clockwise pattern.

An A3 report typically includes (in clockwise order) a description of the project and situation (background, current state, and impact), identification of root causes (analysis), corrective recommendations to achieve resolution of the problem (the objective and future state), and an action/implementation plan with tracking (follow-up).

In addition to its use for problem-solving activities, the A3 report can also be used to structure thinking for status reports and proposals. It is deceptively simple. When done correctly, the A3 report is considered a basic communication tool that is succinct and adds value through storytelling, root-cause analysis, and scientific thinking.

P l a n	Do
	Check
	Act

Figure 5.4 A3 report format.

Title

Date

Background	Proposal
Current Conditions	Plan
Goal	
Analysis	Follow-up

Figure 5.5 A3 report template.

Infographics

An infographic is essentially a project dashboard report on steroids. In an infographic, many different pieces of information about a single topic (in this case, perhaps the project, program, or portfolio) are described using text and several different types of visuals, arranged in a layout to form a single-page poster-type narrative. Visuals may include maps, illustrations, and/or photographs, along with text, tables, and charts.

Because an infographic is so graphic and information-intensive, it is not a style suited to frequently issued reports. It is perhaps best suited to annual reports, or special reports to stakeholders. Due to its engaging and appealing layout, an infographic is most useful when communicating project information to a public, or very broad, audience, as a poster or an editorial illustration.

The infographic below depicts the phases of a typical construction project lifecycle. Each project phase is color-coded. A legend describes the project management services required during each project phase.

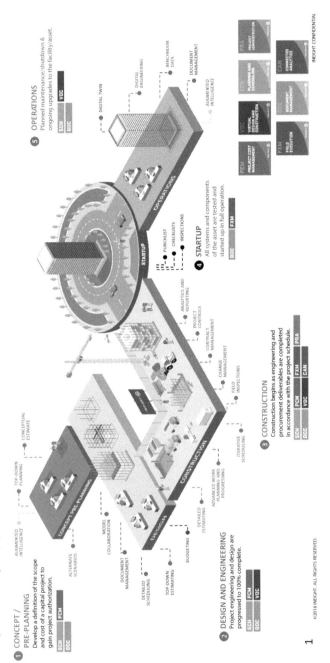

Timely, accurate, and integrated project information is required to achieve confidence and clarity across the entire capital project life cycle.

① CONCEPT / PRE-PLANNING
Develop a definition of the scope and cost of a capital project to gain project authorization.

SCH PCM
DOC

AUGMENTED INTELLIGENCE
TOP-DOWN PLANNING
ALTERNATE SCENARIOS
CONCEPTUAL ESTIMATE

② DESIGN AND ENGINEERING
Project engineering and design are progressed to 100% complete.

SCH PCM
DOC VDC

DETAILED SCHEDULING
TOP-DOWN ESTIMATING
BUDGETING
DETAILED ESTIMATING
DOCUMENT MANAGEMENT
MODEL COLLABORATION

CONCEPT PRE-PLANNING
DESIGN
CONSTRUCTION
STARTUP
OPERATIONS

ADVANCED WORK PLANNING AND PROGRESSING
ITERATIVE SCHEDULING
FIELD INSPECTIONS
CHANGE MANAGEMENT
CONTRACT MANAGEMENT
PROJECT CONTROLS
ANALYTICS AND REPORTING

③ CONSTRUCTION
Construction begins as engineering and procurement deliverables are completed in accordance with the project schedule.

SCH PCM FXM PRA
DOC VDC CAN

PUNCHLIST
CHECKLISTS
INSPECTIONS

④ STARTUP
All systems and components of the asset are tested and started up in full operation.

DOC FXM

DIGITAL ENGINEERING
DIGITAL TWIN
BENCHMARK DATA
DOCUMENT MANAGEMENT
AUGMENTED INTELLIGENCE

⑤ OPERATIONS
Planned maintenance/shutdown & ongoing upgrades to the facility/asset.

SCH VDC
DOC

PCM PROJECT COST MANAGEMENT
VDC VIRTUAL AND DESIGN CONSTRUCTION
FXM FIELD EXECUTION

SCH SCHEDULING AND CONSTRUCTION
DOC DOCUMENT MANAGEMENT
PRA PROJECT ADMINISTRATION
CAN CONNECTED ANALYTICS

INEIGHT CONFIDENTIAL

©2018 INEIGHT. ALL RIGHTS RESERVED.

1

Figure 5.6 Infographic example.

Source: Graphic provided by InEight, using InEight Basis software.

Infographics created for a website gain additional capabilities due to the extra dimensions inherent to the platform. On a website, infographics may be animated and/or interactive. Interactive infographics allow the viewer to explore data more deeply, or be guided through a story or narrative.

An infographic is a special-purpose report that is issued on an infrequent basis. Stakeholders who find an infographic beneficial will include external stakeholders, such as the general public, and special-purpose governing boards, such as a community oversight committee.

Metric reports

Metrics are a proxy for the description of project status, a set of measurements by which success, benefits realization, and milestone achievement can be assessed and acted upon. They are often included in project reports and project dashboards as a quantitative measure of past and current performance. Metrics and key performance indicators (KPI) are derived from critical success factors (CSF), which are typically aligned with project goals and organizational strategy. Metrics are an easy way to quantify project status, compare information between projects, and create a historical record. Metrics are useful for project monitoring, reporting the project status at that moment.

Metrics to be reported may include:

- Cost deviation
- Schedule deviation
- Achievement of milestones
- Units completed
- Work effort
- Percentage complete
- Cycle time
- Production rates
- Reliability
- Defect rates
- Number of open issues
- Quality
- Safety

In addition to stand-alone reports (such as dashboard reports), metrics frequently appear within other project reports such as the project status, schedule, cost, quality, safety, and risk reports. Metrics may be static or dynamic. With a static metric, the goal is to achieve the metric value during each period. For dynamic metrics, the goal is for the team to iterate toward the agreed-upon metric, achieving measurable progress during each period.

In the metric report example shown below, a tabular form is used to show the status of each KPI metric. A stoplight system is used to illustrate the urgency of each metric.

As noted in several instances below, metric reports translate well to a dashboard format.

In the metric report example shown below, various targets are shown, including meters of pipe installed per piece of equipment, the schedule performance index, the monetary value of open commitments, the proportion of contingency returned to the owner because it was unused, the changes in productivity, and the number of engineering hours expended per piece of equipment.

Metrics are often included in reports that are issued on an annual, monthly, and milestone (or stage-gate) basis, but may also be produced at any time, as needed. Stakeholders who look to metrics to gauge the health of the project include: governing boards, project sponsors, project executives, program and project managers, contractors, insurers, and more.

If the purpose of metrics and data sources is not adequately explained, metrics can easily be misunderstood and misused or misquoted. They must be quantifiable, actionable, and relevant to the project objectives. How the metrics were developed, what benchmarking was performed, what is included or excluded in the calculation, and their relevance to the project or organization must be carefully described, transparent, and available on demand.

Project KPI Summary
Sheet Edit Display Rows

Group: KPI Group	KPI Name	Not Tracking	At Risk	Tracking
01 Cost				
	03 Forecast Variance	0	1	5
	01 On Budget	1	0	5
	02 Budget Variance	0	1	5
	04 CPI	6	0	0
02 Schedule				
	02 SPI	6	0	0
	01 On Schedule	0	0	6
03 Control				
	04 Risk Score	0	1	5
	03 Open Risks	0	2	4
	02 Open Issues	0	2	4
	01 Open Changes	0	1	5

Rows 1 - 13 of 13   Show All Page Size 20

Figure 5.7 Metric report example.

Source: Graphic provided by Hexagon, using EcoSys software.

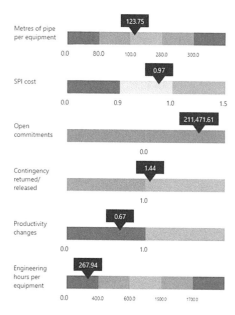

Figure 5.8 Metric report example #2.

Source: Graphic provided by Cost Engineering Consultancy, using Cleopatra Enterprise software.

One of the challenges with metrics is that they can inspire bad behavior just as much as they inspire good behavior. Project team members tend to focus on and perform to the metrics, potentially overlooking areas of the project that require attention and management. Further, metrics that are tied to incentives create a situation ripe for strategic deception and gaming. KPIs must be clearly linked to driving successful project outcomes.

Another challenge with metrics is that they must be very carefully defined for the specific project and the project phase, and must be constantly monitored, lest they unintentionally create a skewed perspective on the project. For example, metrics that are appropriate at the start of the project might not be as meaningful during periods of significant change and risk. They may become obsolete, or less meaningful over time. Metrics that are appropriate for one project might not be as relevant on another project. They are a proxy for measurement of success, and care must be taken to ensure they report not just what can be measured but what should be measured directly and consistently. As such, metrics should be reevaluated on a periodic basis for suitability and appropriateness.

Project health check

Project health checks are not well defined in the business world, and are often a product of consultant work that focuses more on the organization and governance than on the project. The intent of the project health check is to report more deeply and broadly than the traditional KPIs of time, cost, and quality. A typical project health check relies heavily on the use of metrics and "best practice" checklists, focusing on the creation and use of project management procedures.

A dashboard-style report format is useful for project health checks, especially where metrics are presented as graphics.

Balanced scorecard

Another type of metric report is the project-level balanced scorecard. A balanced scorecard is a way of comparing the business strategy development process with the strategic deployment process, focusing on the successful achievement of business objectives. On a project, this scorecard can help ensure that the project scope and activities align with organizational strategy. The report typically measures key performance indicators in the categories of both business metrics or requirements (customers, growth) and traditional financial metrics.

A dashboard-style report format is useful for balanced scorecards, especially where KPIs are presented as graphics.

Benchmarking

Benchmarking is often used to compare one organization to another, projects against those of competitors or peers, or existing processes against best practices. It is done to identify and establish goals. A benchmarked comparison assessment can be used to evaluate project line items, milestones, and change, and can also be used to measure continuous improvement within an organization. For the purposes of this book, benchmarking is discussed in the context of comparing projects against other projects within the same organizational portfolio or program. As the objective is to compare "apples to apples," the outputs typically focus on simple historical data such as: unit costs, units of time, and quantities installed or output.

There are, of course, challenges and risks. As with metrics, benchmarked performance data must be transparent and adequately explained. The projects benchmarked must be similar enough to be meaningfully compared. Benchmarking relies heavily on reported data; of critical importance is a thorough understanding of what information is included or excluded in the reports, the data source, and the quality and reliability of information obtained. Assumptions about common definitions, terminology, categorization, and consistency in data collection may be incorrect, which is especially dangerous and risky when used retrospectively and out of context. The information utilized must be reproducible and thoroughly documented, with an understanding of context and history. Information on past projects may also be out of date, requiring cost escalation or location indexing for the benchmarked data to be brought to parity for comparison with current projects. Finally, just because "it" (a process, strategy, or best practice) worked for competitors, does not necessarily mean it will work for everybody; beware that which is benchmarked.

Formats for benchmark reports vary, and typically include narrative, statistics, and graphics. Figure 5.15 is a schedule benchmarking report.

Benchmarking is often included in special-purpose reports. Stakeholders that use benchmarked information include: governing boards, project sponsors, project executives, program and project managers, risk officers, government agencies, financiers, and insurers.

Project status reports

The project status report is a heavily narrative report that communicates the ongoing progress of the project. Due to the amount of content included, project status reports can be voluminous. Information provided often follows a specific template, to ensure a consistent format from period to period. The project status report may be a contractually required deliverable, and is an important project record. Metrics reported may mirror those used in a one-page dashboard report.

Narrative and statistics typically included in a periodic project report are:

- Executive summary
- Current period activity
- Significant accomplishments
- Planned activities
- Cost status
- Schedule status
- Testing results
- Open issues
- Action items
- Photos

A project status report is often issued on an annual, monthly, milestone, and stage-gate basis, but may also be produced more frequently as needed.

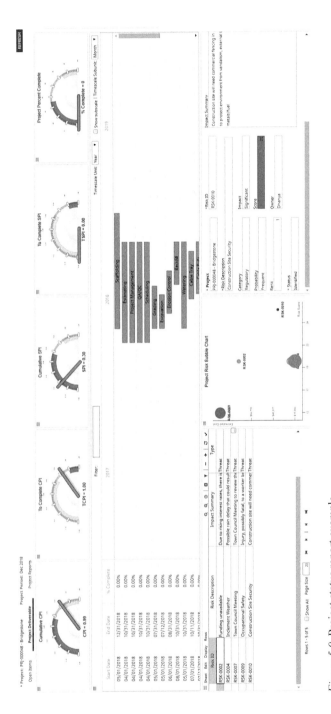

Figure 5.9 Project status report example.

Source: Graphic provided by Hexagon, using EcoSys software.

Most internal stakeholders will receive the project status report, and distribution may include interested parties such as regulatory, licensing, and government agencies, financiers, and insurers.

The project status report shown above is a dashboard-style report that provides high-level statistics about the project. The primary focus of the report is on project schedule percentage complete by activity. Cost and schedule performance indices, and percentage complete, are shown as radial gauges. The report also includes risks, shown in both tabular and bubble chart format.

Program and portfolio

A project may also be part of a bigger program of grouped, related projects, or a corporate portfolio. Within a program, projects are managed in a coordinated fashion according to the same governance structure and processes, thus sharing resources. Like the projects it encapsulates, a program is a temporary organization. Within a portfolio, related and non-related projects are identified, categorized, and prioritized according to corporate strategic objectives. Program-level and portfolio-level reporting requirements differ from project-level reporting in the level of detail provided about individual projects.

The portfolio overview report shown below is a dashboard-style report that lists the projects contained within the portfolio, along with relevant high-level statistics (start date, end date, location, and industry). It includes a simplified schedule bar chart, and a table with select cost, resource, and revenue data.

The format of a program- or portfolio-status report may be very similar to a status report for a project, with data aggregated for the program or portfolio.

A program- or portfolio-level status report is often issued on an annual and monthly basis, but may also be produced more frequently as needed. Most internal stakeholders will receive this status report, and distribution may include interested parties such as regulatory, licensing, and government agencies, financiers, and insurers.

Pipeline

A pipeline report is a type of project tracker that can be used to display various types of project information. It is a useful prioritization tool for resource and cash flow management.

A dashboard format can be used to graphically communicate the status or stage of different projects in a program or portfolio, with additional information provided as narrative or tables.

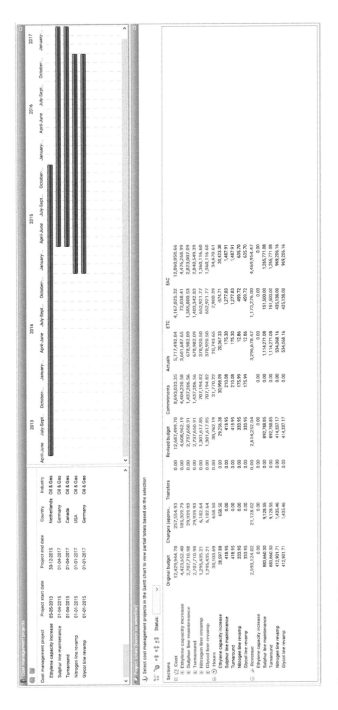

Figure 5.10 Portfolio overview report example.

Source: Graphic provided by Cost Engineering Consultancy, using Cleopatra Enterprise software.

A pipeline report is often issued on a bi-weekly basis, for hands-on project management. Stakeholders interested in a pipeline report typically include the project sponsor, program and project managers, and project team members within the PMO.

Progress, plans, and problems

An oft-used management technique for periodic status reports, especially those that occur frequently, is to focus on the identification of accomplishments (progress), next steps or objectives (plans), and issues that require resolution (problems). Such reports are simple, require little time to write, and do not rely heavily on graphics or formatting. Each category of progress, plans, and problems simply contains a list of bullet point items. It is an efficient way to convey status and other relevant information.

Some projects, especially those following an agile methodology, encourage daily reporting or a daily stand-up. These reports are intended to create a level of transparency in project management. The progress, plans, and problems format is ideal for this type of reporting.

A progress, plans, and problems report is often issued on a weekly or bi-weekly basis, for hands-on project management. Stakeholders interested in a progress, plans, and problems report typically include the project sponsor, program and project managers, and project team members within the PMO.

Sprint review

A sprint review is typically a dashboard or overview issued at the end of a scrum project sprint. The report is a tool for soliciting feedback before the next sprint. It should include fundamental project status information, such as achievements, backlog, and burndown.

This type of report could follow a progress, plans, and problems format, with additional graphics.

Stakeholders interested in a sprint review typically include the project sponsor, project and organizational executives, program and project managers, and project team members within the PMO. The audience may include governing boards, government agencies, financiers, and insurers as needed.

End-of-project

An end-of-project (also project final, or project closeout) report is the last status report to be generated for a project. It is used to document the achievements of the project, and evaluate performance. The report may be a contractually required deliverable, and is an important project record.

This type of report will typically follow the format of a project status report, with additional information (such as closeout and lessons learned).

Most internal stakeholders will receive the project status report, and distribution may include interested parties such as regulatory, licensing, and government agencies, financiers, and insurers. The report is an important part of the project's historic record.

Management controls reporting

Management controls includes all project management, project controls, and related governance, including the management of, and compliance with, processes, policies, and procedures. Cost, schedule, and quality tend to be the primary focus of reports from management controls.

Cost

Once the project estimate has quantified, costed, and priced the resources required to deliver the project in accordance with technical and programmatic requirements, a project budget is created. This is the amount against which project performance is measured. Approved changes are incorporated into the cost control basis as they occur.

A project cost report and baseline are important project records. The most common cost report involves a comparison of the current cost to the baseline (original approved) or target cost. The current cost reflects not just actual expenditures as of the current date, but the revised estimate at completion and (often) the estimate at completion (EAC). Cost reports may be produced for any level of detail, such as: activity, work package, project, program, or portfolio. The cost report may also include a frequency analysis of cost changes by category, enabling management to focus on potential problem areas. Metrics reported for cost may include percentage complete, percentage change, difference between budgeted and actual expenditures, and increase or decrease to project budget.

The cost report shown below is a table that provides cost data by contract and supplier. It includes not only the cost baseline (original budget cost), but also approved change orders, commitments, actual expenditures, and forecast.

Again, there is no one way to develop and present a cost report, although there are some elements that will almost always be included. The cost report shown below is a table that also provides cost data by contract and service category. It includes the original budget, pending and forecasted budget changes, commitments, and actuals.

Breakdown structure:	Original budget cost	Approved changes	Revised budget	Commitments (previous month)	Commitments (to date)	Actuals (previous month)	Actuals (to date)	ETC (to date)	EAC (to date)	Cost variance at completion
CBS										
CBS - CBS Cost Engineering										
SBE - Subtotal Base Estimate										
SMC - Subtotals Materials and Construction										
DFM - Direct Furnished Materials										
1000 - Mechanical Equipment	512,160	42,120	554,280	585,720.00	578,980	586,775.00	586,775	7,860	586,840	32,560.00
3000 - Piping Materials	295,573	9,655	305,228	322,410.00	322,410	321,547.50	321,548	1,409	323,819	18,590.45
4000 - Instrumentation Materials	560,800	30,646	591,446	647,318.88	647,319	647,503.88	647,504	1,514	648,833	57,387.38
5000 - Electrical Materials	82,135	12,284	94,418	98,044.69	98,045	98,063.60	98,064	8	98,053	3,634.35
6000 - Miscellaneous Materials	0	0	0	0.00	0	0.00	0	0	0	0.00
DFM - Direct Furnished Materials	1,450,668	94,705	1,545,372	1,653,493.57	1,646,754	1,653,889.98	1,653,890	10,791	1,657,545	112,172.18
DFC - Direct Field Contracts										
7100 - Site Development	24,483	0	24,483	24,700.00	24,700	24,500.00	24,500	14	24,714	230.98
7200 - Piling	0	0	0	0.00	0	0.00	0	0	0	0.00
7300 - Civil	541,006	45,440	586,446	678,050.00	678,050	678,050.00	678,050	1,482	679,532	93,086.02
7400 - Buildings	0	0	0	0.00	0	0.00	0	0	0	0.00
7500 - Structural Steel	150,615	0	150,615	225,615.00	225,615	225,615.00	225,615	0	225,615	75,000.00
7600 - General Mechanical	884,984	36,415	921,399	478,575.46	963,244	329,222.71	667,244	1,223	964,467	43,067.57
7700 - Instrumentation & Electrical	163,482	190	163,672	49,902.73	166,529	16,038.87	166,729	697	167,226	3,554.67
7800 - Safety & Protection	0	0	0	0.00	0	0.00	0	0	0	0.00
7900 - Field Erected Activities	0	0	0	0.00	0	0.00	0	0	0	0.00
DFC - Direct Field Contracts	1,764,570	82,045	1,846,615	1,456,843.19	2,058,138	1,273,426.58	1,762,138	3,416	2,061,554	214,939.25
SMC - Subtotals Materials and Construction	3,215,237	176,750	3,391,987	3,110,336.76	3,704,892	2,927,316.56	3,416,028	14,207	3,719,099	327,111.43
IFC - Subtotal Indirect Field Costs										
8000 - Indirect Costs	678,415	8,560	686,975	686,199.01	692,599	195,305.39	185,660	2,216	694,815	7,840.00
9000 - Other Costs	0	0	0	0.00	0	0.00	0	0	0	0.00
IFC - Subtotal Indirect Field Costs	678,415	8,560	686,975	686,199.01	692,599	195,305.39	185,660	2,216	694,815	7,840.00
SBE - Subtotal Base Estimate	3,893,652	185,310	4,078,962	3,796,535.77	4,397,491	3,122,621.95	3,601,688	16,423	4,413,914	334,951.43
9800 - Escalation	130,000	0	130,000	0.00	0	0.00	0	10,400	10,400	-119,600.00
9900 - Contingency	400,000	0	400,000	0.00	0	0.00	0	52,000	52,000	-348,000.00
CBS - CBS Cost Engineering	4,423,652	185,310	4,608,962	3,796,535.77	4,397,491	3,122,621.95	3,601,688	78,823	4,476,314	-132,648.57
Unassigned	0	0	0	0.00	0	0.00	0	0	0	0.00
Grand total	4,423,652	185,310	4,608,962	3,796,535.77	4,397,491	3,122,621.95	3,601,688	78,823	4,476,314	-132,648.57

Figure 5.11 Cost report example.

Source: Graphic provided by Cost Engineering Consultancy, using Cleopatra Enterprise software.

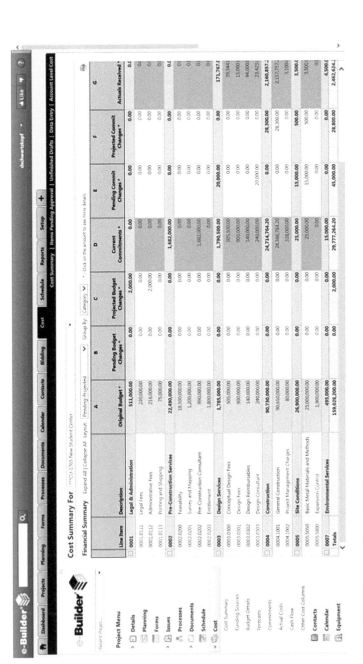

Figure 5.12 Cost report example #2.

Source: Graphic provided by e-Builder (A Trimble Company), using e-Builder Enterprise software.

The cost report shown above provides budget, change, commitment, and forecast data in a tabular format. It also includes dashboard-type elements, such as a bar and line chart showing the same information graphically, both by month and cumulatively.

As with the project status report, a cost report is often issued on an annual, monthly, milestone, and stage-gate basis, but may also be produced more frequently as needed. Most internal stakeholders will receive the cost report, and distribution may include other external interested parties.

Schedule

The project schedule is the product of the planning of project work over the timeline of the project. During the development of the schedule, the project is defined as a series of activities and tasks that are then put into sequence, each with its own start date, finish date, and duration. Relationships (logic) between the activities are defined, in terms of precedence and concurrence, and time constraints and major project milestones added. Every schedule will have a critical path, the longest path in the schedule, wherein any change to activities on the critical path will directly impact the project deliverable date. A resource-loaded schedule with finite resources and resource dependencies can be used to identify the critical chain.

A project schedule report and a schedule baseline are important project records. Schedules may be very simple, merely a specialized bar chart (Gantt chart) showing major activities and completion date, or may be much more complicated. Sophisticated schedules include coding to indicate loading of costs and resources for scheduled activities, consideration of long-lead items, congestion of activities, criticality, cash flow, and capacity of vendors, suppliers, contractors, and subcontractors. Approved changes are incorporated into the schedule control basis.

As noted earlier, the most common schedule report involves a comparison of the current schedule to the baseline (original approved) or target schedule, and achievement of key milestones. The current schedule reflects not just actual achievement and progress as of the current date, but the revised schedule going forward to completion. Changes to scheduled activities might or might not impact the planned completion date of the project, depending on whether or not those activities reside on the critical path. Schedule reports may be produced for any level of schedule detail, such as: activity, work package, project, program, or portfolio. The schedule report may also include a frequency analysis of schedule changes by category, enabling management to focus on potential problem areas.

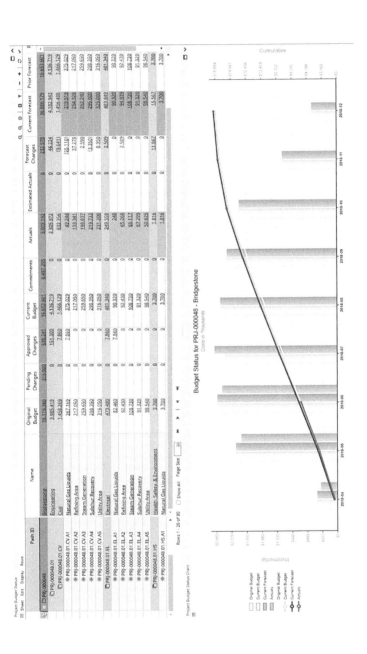

Figure 5.13 Cost report example #3.

Source: Graphic provided by Hexagon using EcoSys software.

Metrics reported for schedule may include percent completion for the project and activities, number of tasks completed, tasks not started, tasks in process, tasks completed, and more. Specialty schedule reports include a weekly or bi-weekly look-ahead at scheduled activities. A baseline schedule and periodic schedule status report may comprise contractually required deliverables.

The traditional schedule report below demonstrates time-based relationships between a series of sequenced activities and tasks. Data shown includes start date, finish date, and duration. The critical path is shown in red.

Again, there is no one way to develop and present a schedule. The schedule report below compares actual schedule progress against a benchmark, for various design, fabrication, procurement, and construction activities.

As with the project status report, a schedule report is often issued on an annual, monthly, milestone, and stage-gate basis, but may also be produced more frequently as needed. Most internal stakeholders will receive the schedule report, and distribution may include other interested external parties.

Figure 5.14   Schedule report example.

Source: Graphic provided by Hexagon using EcoSys software.

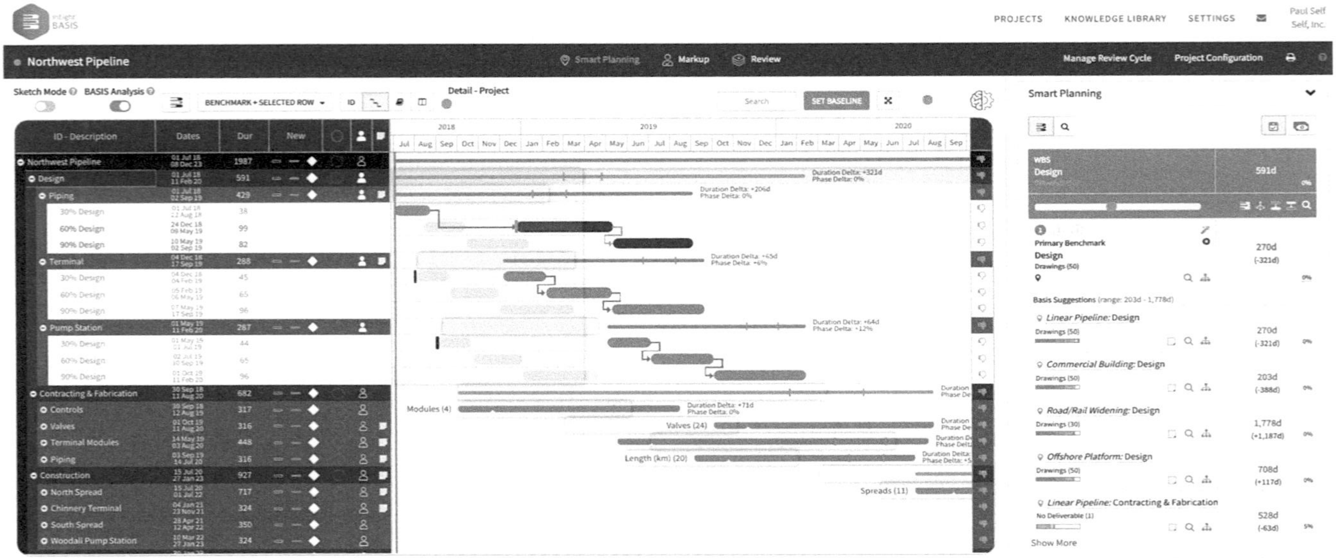

Figure 5.15 Schedule report example #2.

Source: Graphic provided by InEight, using InEight Basis software.

Resources

A resource report is used to track and/or forecast the capacity and/or utilization of project resources, usually staff resources, by task or activity. However, resource reports can be used for many different kinds of project resources, including project funding (known as a cash flow report), contractors, tools, and equipment. A resource report may be an output from a resource-loaded schedule. Figures 5.16 and 5.17 are resource reports that focus specifically on cash flow.

A resource report is often issued on a monthly basis, but may be produced more frequently as needed. Stakeholders interested in a resource report typically include the project sponsor, project and organizational executives, program and project managers, and project team members within the PMO. The audience may include governing boards and financiers, as needed.

Cash flow

Cash flow projections represent a forecasted expenditure profile for the project, balancing expected timing and magnitude of expenditures. Cash flow projections may also include anticipated income. A gap between expenditures and income represents a potential need for financing. Using inputs from a resource-loaded schedule, cash flow may serve as a basis for appropriations requests, phased decision-making, earned value calculations, and cost management.

A cash flow report is a special kind of resource report. Cash flow may be represented as a chart, or as a table.

The cash flow graphic below represents an idealized forecast of cash flow for a project, before any expenditures have been incurred. Note that the cumulative spend overlay is an S-curve.

The cash flow plot shown below graphs both cash in and actual costs, including an overlay for cumulative spend. It has two axes, one for cash flow value and one for cumulative spend, and a vertical line to mark the distinction between actual and projected cash flows.

A cash flow report is often issued on an annual and monthly basis, but may be produced more frequently as needed. Stakeholders interested in a cash flow report typically include the project sponsor, project and organizational executives (especially the CFO), program and project managers, and project team members within the PMO. The audience may include governing boards, government agencies, and financiers, as needed.

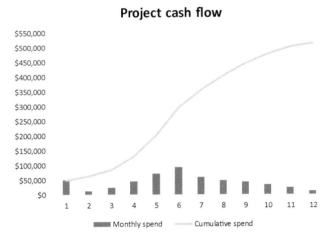

Figure 5.16 Cash flow report example, forecasted.

Source: This cash flow diagram is a bar chart, with a project S-curve overlay for cumulative spend.

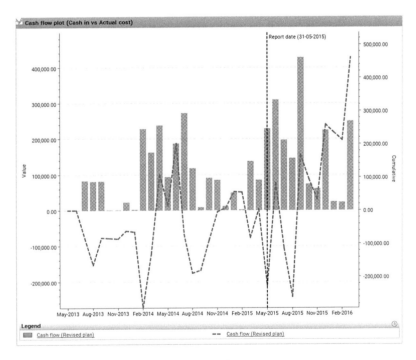

Figure 5.17 Cash flow report example, actual.

Source: Graphic provided by Cost Engineering Consultancy, using Cleopatra Enterprise software.

Procurement

The project procurement process includes identifying and then planning for the purchase of items required by the project. Procurement may require a formal, transparent process of selection, which includes the receipt and comparative review of proposals and bids.

A procurement report is often used to show the status of progress regarding contracts and purchase orders issued, invoices received, invoices paid, and other related information. Included in the report will be vendors, fabricators, suppliers, contractors, and subcontractors.

Care must be taken during reporting to ensure items procured by the project team are not commingled in reporting with items procured by the owner organization. This could lead to duplication or omission of purchased items in the report, especially where project and procurement reports are separate.

A procurement report is often issued on a monthly and bi-weekly basis, but may be produced more frequently as needed. Stakeholders interested in a procurement report typically include the project sponsor, project and organizational executives, program and project managers, and project team members within the PMO.

Quality

Quality assurance and quality control (QA/QC) are tasked with identifying deviations from specifications and/or standards, and ensuring project deliverables meet established performance, objectives, and requirements. Quality assurance (QA) focuses on process, while quality control (QC) focuses on product. A quality management plan will likely include independent verification and validation (IV&V). Quality issues may be identified during any phase of the project lifecycle, and occur most frequently during execution. Quality reporting includes quality plan metrics, statistics regarding deviations, root-cause analyses, and may also include defect trend reports and process improvement plans.

A quality report is often issued on a monthly and bi-weekly basis, but may be produced more frequently as needed. Stakeholders interested in a procurement report typically include the project sponsor, project and organizational executives, program and project managers, and project team members within the PMO. The audience may include governing boards, regulatory, licensing, and government agencies, financiers and insurers, and select contractors, vendors, and suppliers.

Change/variance

Approved change orders become part of the contract documents, and contribute to the revised cost baseline. The change-reporting process includes the tracking and categorization of changes by impact, type, and causation, and also includes information on the status of change approvals. Keep in mind, change reporting often reports only that change happened. It might group changes by type, but it does not typically provide more granular or greatly detailed information about why performance differed from what was expected, or what caused the change, unless a more detailed report is produced.

Some change reports take the form of an administrative change log, to track forecasted, received, and approved change requests. Layers of definition and categorization can be used to aggregate changes by type, enabling stakeholder focus in specific areas, and deeper analytics. Metrics included

Breakdown structure: CBS	Original budget cost	Approved changes	Pending Changes	Revised budget
⊟ CBS - CBS Cost Engineering				
⊟ SBE - Subtotal Base Estimate				
⊟ SMC - Subtotals Materials and Construction				
⊟ DFM - Direct Furnished Materials				
⊞ 1000 - Mechanical Equipment	512,160	42,120	0.00	554,280
⊞ 3000 - Piping Materials	295,573	9,655	0.00	305,228
⊞ 4000 - Instrumentation Materials	560,800	30,646	0.00	591,446
⊞ 5000 - Electrical Materials	82,135	12,284	0.00	94,418
⊞ 6000 - Miscellaneous Materials	0	0	0.00	0
DFM - Direct Furnished Materials	1,450,668	94,705	0.00	1,545,372
⊟ DFC - Direct Field Contracts				
⊞ 7100 - Site Development	24,483	0	0.00	24,483
7200 - Piling	0	0	0.00	0
⊞ 7300 - Civil	541,006	45,440	0.00	586,446
⊞ 7400 - Buildings	0	0	0.00	0
⊞ 7500 - Structural Steel	150,615	0	0.00	150,615
⊞ 7600 - General Mechanical	884,984	36,415	0.00	921,399
⊞ 7700 - Instrumentation & Electrical	163,482	190	0.00	163,672
⊞ 7800 - Safety & Protection	0	0	0.00	0
⊞ 7900 - Field Erected Activities	0	0	0.00	0
DFC - Direct Field Contracts	1,764,570	82,045	0.00	1,846,615
SMC - Subtotals Materials and Construction	3,215,237	176,750	0.00	3,391,987
⊟ IFC - Subtotal Indirect Field Costs				
⊟ 8000 - Indirect Costs				
⊞ 8100 - Definition Costs	144,686	8,560	0.00	153,246
⊞ 8200 - Project Management	77,166	0	0.00	77,166
⊞ 8300 - Engineering	321,524	0	0.00	321,524
⊞ 8400 - Construction Management & Commissioning	128,610	0	0.00	128,610
8500 - Start-Up	6,430	0	0.00	6,430
⊞ 8700 - Facilities	0	0	0.00	0
8800 - Contractor Mark-Ups (Overhead, Profit, Risk)	0	0	0.00	0
8000 - Indirect Costs	678,415	8,560	0.00	686,975
⊞ 9000 - Other Costs	0	0	0.00	0
IFC - Subtotal Indirect Field Costs	678,415	8,560	0.00	686,975
SBE - Subtotal Base Estimate	3,893,652	185,310	0.00	4,078,962
9800 - Escalation	130,000	0	0.00	130,000
9900 - Contingency	400,000	0	0.00	400,000
CBS - CBS Cost Engineering	4,423,652	185,310	0.00	4,608,962

Figure 5.18 Change report example.

Source: Graphic provided by Cost Engineering Consultancy, using Cleopatra Enterprise software.

in the report may include the number of new/open/closed change requests, percentage of cost and schedule change, and statistical data on change validation and analysis. Key to the usefulness of a change report is timeliness and early identification of change.

The change report shown above is in the form of a table, and represents a simplified version of the cost report shown above, focusing solely on the original budgeted cost of the project, approved change orders, pending changes, and the revised budget.

A change report is often issued on a monthly, bi-weekly, milestone, or stage-gate basis, but may be produced more frequently as needed. Stakeholders interested in a change report typically include the project sponsor, project and organizational executives, program and project managers, and project team members within the PMO. The audience may include governing boards, regulatory, licensing, and government agencies, financiers and insurers, and select contractors, vendors, and suppliers.

Variance analysis

Variance analysis is the computation and reporting of circumstances or behavior that are different than planned. On projects, this is typically applied to the overall cost and schedule, but may also be performed for planned vs. actual work, discrete elements (such as unit prices, overhead costs, and efficiency), metrics, and characteristics of the project deliverables. Not all variances are material; change won't necessarily always impact the project final cost and critical path.

Variance reporting often plots what has happened on a project against a curve representing what was expected to occur, or may show data in a tabular or bar chart format. It can be used to distinguish trends from random change, and leads to root-cause analysis and corrective action plans. Variance analysis is also a product of earned value management.

The variance analysis graphic below shows the baseline project cost and final project cost as columns, with variances grouped by trade.

A variance analysis is often issued on an as-needed basis. Stakeholders interested in a variance analysis typically include the project sponsor, project and organizational executives, program and project managers, and project team members within the PMO. The audience may include governing boards, regulatory, licensing, and government agencies, financiers and insurers, and select contractors, vendors, and suppliers.

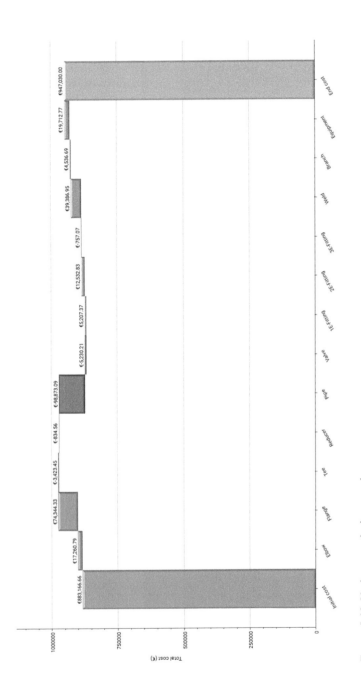

Figure 5.19 Variance analysis example.

Source: Graphic provided by Cost Engineering Consultancy, using Cleopatra Enterprise software.

Earned value

Variance analysis is often applied in earned value (EV) reporting. Earned value is a progress monitoring and performance measurement tool that integrates schedule, budget, actual, and percentage complete data on a weighted progress basis, to compare actual and planned work performance and the effort required. It can also be used to forecast the project outcome, and may be a component in stage-gate analysis. Both cost-based and schedule-based earned value analysis can be performed.

The earned value report below (Figure 5.20) uses a tabular format to list project activities and percent complete.

The bubble chart shown (Figure 5.21) below plots schedule (SPI) and cost (CPI) performance indices of certain project line items, including activities by trade (subcontractor), major equipment, and owner cost.

The schedule status report below (Figure 5.22) shows schedule performance index (SPI) over time. An SPI of greater than one (positive) indicates more work was accomplished than was planned. A vertical line marks the date of the report.

An earned value report is often issued on a monthly basis, but may also be produced on-demand for specific meetings. Due to the technical content and complexity of the report, the stakeholder audience is often limited to the project sponsor, project executives, program and project managers, and project team members within the PMO.

Issue management

Lists of issues and requests for information (RFI) are all indicators of potential change on the project. An issue log can be used to document and track the status of identified issues; risks are not the same as issues and are reported separately. Reporting on issues enables the project team to focus resources on their mitigation and resolution. Issues may be managed in a database, or tracked on a spreadsheet or by hand. An issue management report will typically describe the issue and its potential impact, category, priority, the date it was identified, name of a person responsible for managing the issue, targeted resolution date, and the date it was resolved. The report may further discuss resolution plans and alternatives. The risk register shown in Figure 5.28 is an example of an issue management report.

An issue log is often prepared on a monthly or bi-weekly basis, but may also be produced more frequently as needed. The stakeholder audience is often limited to the project sponsor, project and organizational executives, program and project managers, and project team members within the PMO, but may also include governing boards.

Earned Value Summary

Path ID	Name	BAC Hours	BAC Cost	Progress Method	Physical % Complete	Preview % Complete	% Complete	Earned Hours	Earned Cost	Earned Percent
PRJ-000048	Bridgestone	86,302	16,653,601				0.0	24,478	4,975,749	29
PRJ-000048.01	Engineering	33,004	4,136,719				0.0	17,951	2,234,001	54
PRJ-000048.01.CV	Civil	11,581	1,466,129				0.0	6,250	781,643	53
PRJ-000048.01.CV.A1	Natural Gas Liquids	2,815	375,029	Weighted Deliverables	0.0	12.9	0.0	363	48,379	13
PRJ-000048.01.CV.A2	Refining Area	1,754	217,050	Weighted Milestones	0.0	55.0	0.0	965	119,378	55
PRJ-000048.01.CV.A3	Steam Generation	2,074	259,650	Physical % Complete	76.0	76.0	0.0	1,576	197,334	76
PRJ-000048.01.CV.A4	Sulphur Recovery	2,384	298,350	Physical % Complete	75.0	75.0	0.0	1,788	223,763	75
PRJ-000048.01.CV.A5	Utility Area	2,554	316,050	Physical % Complete	61.0	61.0	0.0	1,558	192,791	61
PRJ-000048.01.EL	Electrical	4,034	481,340				0.0	2,111	251,107	52
PRJ-000048.01.EL.A1	Natural Gas Liquids	751	90,320	Physical % Complete	0.0	0.0	0.0	0	0	0
PRJ-000048.01.EL.A2	Refining Area	778	92,430	Physical % Complete	69.0	69.0	0.0	537	63,777	69
PRJ-000048.01.EL.A3	Steam Generation	901	108,730	Physical % Complete	53.0	53.0	0.0	478	57,627	53
PRJ-000048.01.EL.A4	Sulphur Recovery	775	91,320	Physical % Complete	87.0	87.0	0.0	674	79,448	87
PRJ-000048.01.EL.A5	Utility Area	829	98,540	Physical % Complete	51.0	51.0	0.0	422	50,255	51
PRJ-000048.01.HS	Health, Safety, & Environment	37	3,700				0.0	19	1,887	51
PRJ-000048.01.HS.A1	Natural Gas Liquids	37	3,700	Physical % Complete	51.0	51.0	0.0	19	1,887	51
PRJ-000048.01.HS.A2	Refining Area	0	0	Physical % Complete	0.0	0.0	0.0	0	0	
PRJ-000048.01.HS.A3	Steam Generation	0	0	Physical % Complete	0.0	0.0	0.0	0	0	
PRJ-000048.01.HS.A4	Sulphur Recovery	0	0	Physical % Complete	0.0	0.0	0.0	0	0	
PRJ-000048.01.HS.A5	Utility Area	0	0	Physical % Complete	0.0	0.0	0.0	0	0	

Rows 1 - 20 of 80   Show All   Page Size 20

Deliverable Register — * Object: A1 - Natural Gas Liquids

Deliverable ID	Deliverable Name	Weight	% Complete	Weighted % Complete
1	General Arrangements	30	43.0	12.9
2	Calcs	40	0.0	0.0
3	Drawings	30	0.0	0.0
		100		12.9

Rows 1 - 3 of 3   Show All   Page Size 20

Deliverable Milestones — Deliverable: 2 - Calcs

ID	Description	Weight	% Complete	Weighted % Complete	EV Deliverable Weighted % Complete
01	Preliminary Calc & Sketch	30	0.0	0.0	0.0
02	Calc & Design	20	0.0	0.0	0.0
03	Back check Calcs	20	0.0	0.0	0.0
04	Final checks	30	0.0	0.0	0.0
		100		0.0	0.0

Rows 1 - 4 of 4   Show All   Page Size 20

Figure 5.20 Earned value report example.

Source: Graphic provided by Hexagon, using EcoSys software.

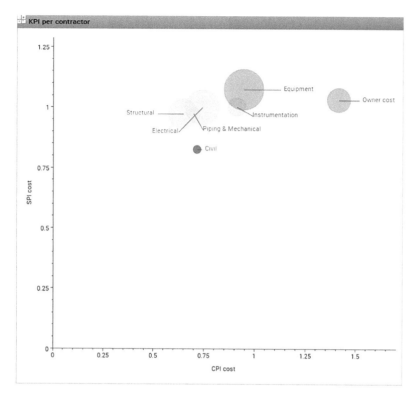

Figure 5.21 Earned value SPI vs. CPI report example.

Source: Graphic provided by Cost Engineering Consultancy, using Cleopatra Enterprise software.

Contingency and reserves

Contingency and reserves are amounts set aside at the start of the project to cover the cost of change. Reporting on the amounts utilized and remaining is a good indicator of whether the project organization can afford more risk or change, and can be used to identify trends in utilization of those funds. At the end of the project, unused funds may be returned to the organization for use on other projects. The contingency and reserves report will typically quantify the original amounts available, amounts expended, and amounts remaining. The report can be segregated by type of contingency and reserves, if that level of detail was provided at the time of budgeting.

The contingency rundown graphic (Figure 5.23) shown below displays the planned contingency drawdown as a curve, compared against actual released and returned costs. A vertical line marks the report date.

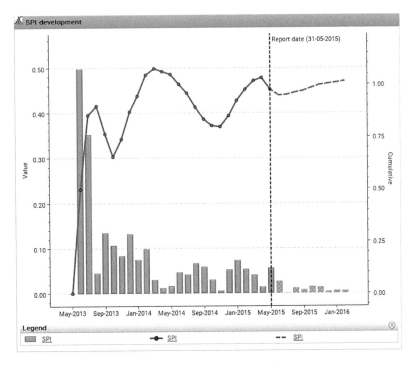

Figure 5.22 Earned value schedule status report example.

Source: Graphic provided by Cost Engineering Consultancy, using Cleopatra Enterprise software.

A contingency log is often prepared on a monthly and bi-weekly basis, but may also be produced more frequently as needed. The stakeholder audience is often limited to the project sponsor, project and organizational executives, program and project managers, and project team members within the PMO, but may also include governing boards.

Forecasting

The majority of project reporting is retrospective, presenting a picture of the current state of the project and what has happened to date. This means actions taken are based on what has happened in the past, not extrapolations of future performance. Certainly, it is easier to take a retroactive look at a project, dissect what happened, and point fingers at the guilty, than to foresee the future. Reliably predicting the future is difficult to do, and project oracles are in short supply.

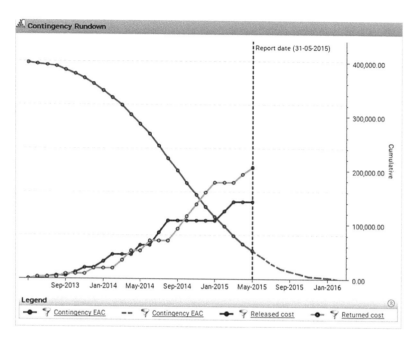

Figure 5.23 Contingency rundown report example.

Source: Graphic provided by Cost Engineering Consultancy, using Cleopatra Enterprise software.

Forecasting reports intend to integrate information about deviations, trends, and change, with a quantification of remaining work. Many elements of the project and investment process require an attempt at forecasting, and there are several ways to approach it. Critical to the quality and usability of the forecasting effort is the availability of data on past and current trends, historic information, and documentation of assumptions. Various types of forecasting reports and mechanisms are described below, and also in the section on risk.

A forecast report is often prepared on a monthly basis, but may also be produced more frequently as needed. The stakeholder audience is often limited to the project sponsor, project and organizational executives, program and project managers, and project team members within the PMO, but may also include governing boards, government agencies, financiers, and insurers.

Estimate at completion

Estimate at completion (EAC) and remaining estimate to complete (ETC) are oft-used proxies for a formal project cost forecast, which considers a current understanding of project risk and productivity. As the project progresses, the project estimate is modified and refined, becoming more definitive. The EAC may be calculated using a formula, or (on a line-item basis) it may be based solely on opinion or hunch. If based on opinion, the number will be heavily reliant on the skill and level of experience of the estimator. As such, the EAC should be treated as a rough forecast, a general indicator that contains inaccuracies.

At the start of the project, before expenditures are incurred, the EAC typically matches the project schedule of values. As change and risk are encountered, the EAC will show variances by line item. Then, as the project proceeds further through its lifecycle, contract amounts are committed, and invoices paid, the difference between the EAC and actual project costs will shrink and approach zero. EAC values are often included in a standard tabular cost report.

The forecast report shown below (Figure 5.24) uses a tabular format to describe each scheduled activity, and then provides forecast data such as EAC and ETC. It also provides cost report information regarding commitments, actuals, percentage complete, and cost performance index.

Forecast information can be conveyed both as data and as a graphic. In the EAC graphic below (Figure 5.25), actual project cost to date is shown to the left of the vertical report date line, and forecasted cost is shown to the right of the line.

Trends

Some project management tools and systems enable limited-range project forecasting by using trend lines to extrapolate future performance and quickly illustrate what has changed since the last report. The assumption is that the project will continue an established pattern of behavior. Such information as the estimate at completion can be plotted over time, resulting in a graphic picture of project performance. Trending may be performed for many elements of project management that have an established baseline, including cost, schedule, quality, variance, and resource utilization. It is recommended to have data from more than a few reporting periods, when calculating trends; more than two points are needed. The trend line will become more refined as more data points are added. Key to the usefulness of a trend report is timeliness and early identification of change.

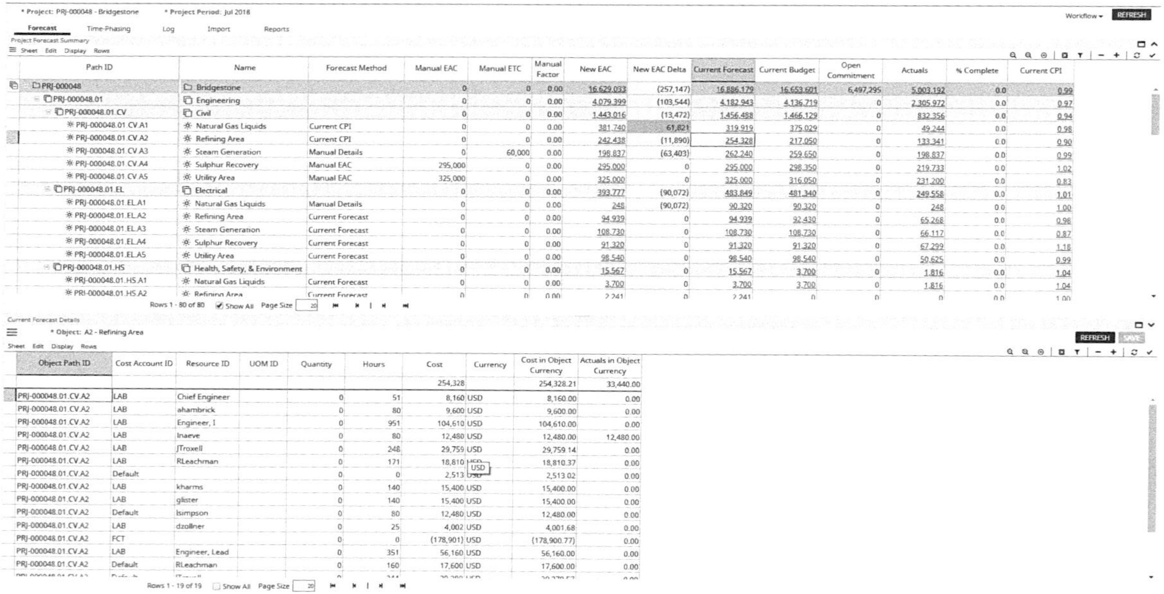

Figure 5.24 Forecast report example.

Source: Graphic provided by Hexagon, using EcoSys software.

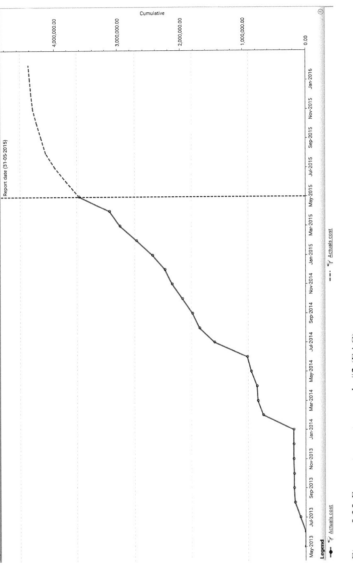

Figure 5.25 Forecast report example #2 (EAC).

Source: Graphic provided by Cost Engineering Consultancy, using Cleopatra Enterprise software.

Extreme care needs to be taken when using trend lines as a forecasting tool, and excessive reliance on such tools is not recommended. Trend lines, as an analytical tool, are easily abused and misused. Use of a trend line assumes project conditions will remain the same, the existing pattern of performance will continue, and the trend line will continue along its charted path. However, project change is a given, and it is reasonable to assume project conditions will not remain the same. Further, projects are complex nonlinear systems that can be easily disrupted by change. As such, trend lines can be used reliably for forecasting in the short term, but those same trend lines are likely to be less reliable if used for long-term projections. Trending is an imperfect art that relies heavily on expert input to predict potential turning points and change.

A trend report is typically issued on-demand for specific meetings. The stakeholder audience is often limited to the project sponsor, project and organizational executives, program and project managers, and project team members within the PMO.

Risk

One of the key elements in both feasibility and forecasting, risk assessment is used to evaluate the project's likelihood of achieving its objectives, by identifying project and enterprise vulnerabilities and opportunities. Risk, for the purposes of this book, is the chance or hazard of commercial loss that occurs by undertaking or failing to undertake a project. Every action (and inaction) has consequences, may impact known risks, and may create new ones. Risk and opportunity are always present; they are multifaceted, inter-dependent, and constantly changing. Risk assessment is a repetitive exercise, because risks constantly change. Risk management is, effectively, an early warning system for project problems. Executive-level stakeholders are increasingly aware of risk, and risk reporting may even be a statutory requirement on the project. Risks can be grouped into various categories, as shown below (Figure 5.26), with examples for each category.

A formal risk management process includes identifying risks and devel-oping a list, then prioritizing those risks according to the level of perceived threat or severity of consequences. Risk assessment relies on professional opinion, which may be the most unreliable part of the risk assessment. Descriptions of risk will be both qualitative and quantitative. Once risks are quantified in terms of probability and impact, they may be modeled using a Monte Carlo technique to calculate recommended contingency and float. Risk identification and management is an iterative process that should be conducted periodically throughout the project lifecycle, to capture risks associated with change.

Technical Risks

- proven / unproven technology
- new product development
- implementation methodology
- equipment and material performance
- planning and design complexity
- commissioning and testing
- evolving requirements
- tie-in to existing project or interface
- scope change
- engineering and design change
- metric vs. imperial measurement
- differing standards
- specialized equipment and materials
- long-lead equipment
- project in an operating facility
- design conflict / interference
- information systems
- scalability
- security vulnerabilities
- technical complexity

Financial and Economic Risks

- inflation
- funding / financing
- market forces
- bidder perception of risk
- labor and material costs and drivers
- labor and material availability
- interest rate
- currency fluctuation
- bankruptcy
- alternative approaches to insurance

Statutory and Political Risks

- local law or government policy
- government influence on disputes
- environmental regulations
- property acquisition
- permitting
- external stakeholder influence
- testing and certification
- official and unofficial holidays
- religious observance
- customs (import / export)
- visas (immigration)

Organizational Risks

- project team capability
- contractor failure
- contractor / vendor / consultant failure or default
- mergers and acquisitions
- staff turnover
- stakeholder turnover
- degree of unfamiliarity
- schedule acceleration
- gaps in responsibility or scope
- communication
- executive support of project
- business processes
- delegated authority
- organizational culture
- reputation

Contractual Risks

- contractual liability
- warranties
- liquidated / consequential / punitive damages
- construction defect
- risk transfer
- conflicting contract language
- inadequate contract protections
- intellectual property
- new contract / delivery method

Other Risks

- climate
- safety
- unknown conditions
- archaeological findings
- contamination
- local customs
- infrastructure
- theft
- translation error
- productivity
- competition

Figure 5.26 Types of risk.

Source: Nalewaik, Alexia and Mills, Anthony (2016). *Project Performance Review: Capturing the Value of Audit, Oversight, and Compliance for Project Success*, p. 58. London: Routledge.

Individual risk analysis and reporting includes a treatment plan for risk reduction, and continuous monitoring of risk change. A sample risk management form is shown below (Figure 5.27).

Once individual risks have been identified and quantified, they can be reported on as a group. Most often, all project risks are shown in a list called a risk register. Metrics captured in a risk report may include the number of new/open/closed risks, and prioritization by probability and impact.

The risk register shown below (Figure 5.28) lists each risk in a tabular format within a database, along with additional information about owner, type, category, status, impact, probability, probable cost impact, and ranking. Each line item can be clicked on to provide even more detailed information on the risk.

There are many different ways to represent risk graphically, each with a specific purpose. Some of these visuals are described below.

A risk report is typically issued monthly and on-demand for specific meetings. The stakeholder audience is often limited to the project sponsor, project and organizational executives, program and project managers, and project team members within the PMO, but may include governing boards, government agencies, financiers, and insurers.

Probability–impact

A probability–impact matrix is a heat map that plots risks against two axes, probability and impact. The matrix can then be used to prioritize risks.

The heat map below (Figurre 5.29) categorizes the impact of risks as low–moderate–high, and probability as unlikely–likely–very likely. Color is used to indicate the seriousness of risks, with the most serious risks in red.

Project S-curve

A project S-curve can be used in many ways; it can be found in reports when illustrating earned value, project progress, cash flow, quantity output, and project schedule. For the purposes of project risk management, the S-curve maps total project cost against probability and is typically an output from a Monte Carlo simulation. The S-curve can be used to determine the amount of contingency to be allocated to the project, depending on the desired level of comfort with the estimate (probability). Contingency is often set at the P80 level (80 percent probability of occurrence), but can be established at any percentage according to the organization's level of risk tolerance.

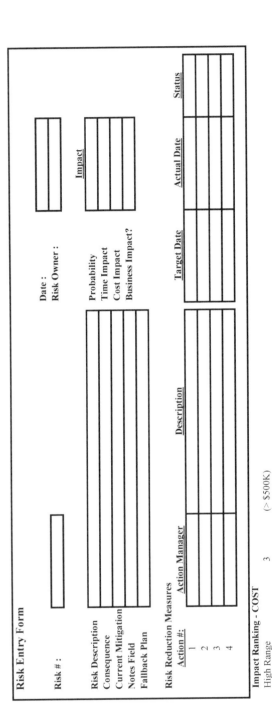

Figure 5.27 Risk management form example.

Source: Nalewaik, Alexia and Mills, Anthony (2016). *Project Performance Review: Capturing the Value of Audit, Oversight, and Compliance for Project Success*, p. 60. London: Routledge.

Figure 5.28 Risk register example.

Source: Graphic provided by Hexagon, using EcoSys software.

	Impact		
	Low	Moderate	High
Very Likely	14	1	10
Likely	1	2	8
Unlikely	5	19	13

(left axis label: **Probability**)

Figure 5.29 Probability–impact matrix example.

In the example shown below (Figure 5.30), contingency is established at P85 (85 percent probability of occurrence). The base estimate is shown as a vertical line, with the Monte Carlo analysis output added as an S-curve overlay. A second vertical line is drawn at the P85 point on the S-curve, establishing the necessary contingency and total forecasted project cost.

Tornado

A "tornado diagram" is a horizontal bar chart that ranks risks in order according to their impact on the project, measured as potential variability. The risks with the highest impact are at the top of the chart, and the remaining risks are ordered according to their forecasted impact. The diagram is an output from sensitivity analysis, part of a Monte Carlo simulation. The same results can also be presented as a spider diagram.

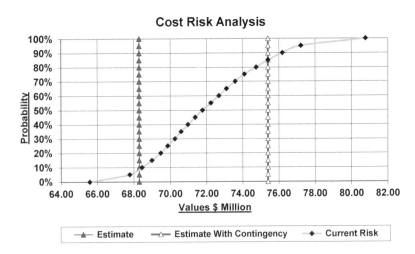

Figure 5.30 Risk S-curve example.

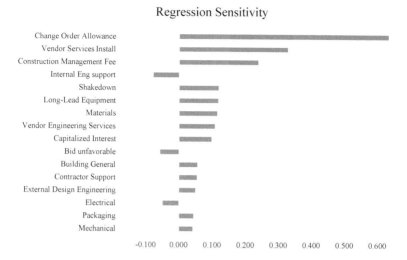

Figure 5.31 Tornado diagram example.

In the tornado diagram shown above (Figure 5.31), expected value is shown on the x-axis, with the individual risks listed above (along the y-axis).

Event chain

An event chain diagram is an advanced type of Gantt (schedule) chart using Monte Carlo simulation, that adds visual information to the schedule risk relationship, such as: threats, opportunities, issues, closed or transferred risks, ripple effects, and more. Events are represented as arrows, with the arrow direction (up or down), size, and color providing information about the risk type (threat or opportunity), probability, and impact. This type of schedule network analysis builds on concepts of critical path and critical chain method scheduling techniques, and endeavors to mitigate biases and improve accuracy in risk assessment.

Stage-gate analysis

Stage-gate analysis (also referred to as phase-gate) is a project assurance tool, designed to improve the likelihood of project success, which combines process and output controls. The stage-gate process is used to contain and control critical phases, deliverables, or milestones in the project.

Stage-gate reviews, also called gateway or phase-gate reviews, occur in sequence at specific decision-making times during the project lifecycle, focusing on achievements, priorities, controls, and risks to successful project delivery.

Areas of assessment will differ from gate to gate, offering an opportunity to realign the project with strategic objectives before continuation. As with metrics, stage-gate requirements need to be very carefully defined and appropriate for both the project and the gate. Stage gates require approval for the project to progress from one stage or phase to the next, else the project may be halted and resource authorizations terminated.

Various types of status reports are issued at regular intervals. They typically include narrative describing the status of objectives (project, stage, or work package), risks, issues, and lessons learned.

- A *highlight report* is a status report that is issued at regular intervals, used to monitor stage and project process.
- A *checkpoint report* is a status report that is specific to work packages.
- The *end project report* is the final report issued for the project, used to communicate project history, performance, and lessons learned. It typically includes a list of project objectives and products, follow-on actions, lessons learned, and comments on team performance.
- An *exception report* is an ad hoc report issued to surface exceptions that may impact success at the next stage, or the project as a whole. It typically identifies exceptions, their root cause, consequences, lessons learned, and recommended action.
- If not included in the end stage or end project reports, *lessons learned* may comprise their own, separate database and log (report).

Internal stakeholders interested in a stage-gate report may include but are not limited to: governing boards, the project or program sponsor, project and organizational executives, project manager, and PMO team members. External stakeholders may include regulatory, licensing, and government agencies, financiers, and insurers.

End stage

An end stage report is typically issued at a stage decision point, providing a description of stage progress. The report may be based on an assurance checklist of key outputs and deliverables. A typical stage-gate report is a summation of the stage review activity, and exception reporting. It includes the status of stage objectives, follow-on actions, risks, issues, lessons learned, and comments on team performance, and identifies objectives for the next stage.

The gate status is often represented by a "stoplight" system of green, yellow, and red. Green indicates the project is generally on target to succeed, yellow indicates there are recommendations that require action and that progress to the next gate is conditional, and red requires immediate attention.

Internal stakeholders interested in a stage-gate report may include but are not limited to: governing boards, the project or program sponsor, project and organizational executives, project manager, and PMO team members. External stakeholders may include regulatory, licensing, and government agencies, financiers, and insurers.

Agile project reports

In addition to the project reports discussed above, there are certain reports that are specific to the agile and scrum styles of project management, often applied on software development projects. Earned value is also used in agile project reporting. Some of these are described below.

- *Work item status* is a narrative status report, table, or information on a project board that shows how many tasks are in progress, and their status.
- *Work item aging* is a table or information on a project board that identifies activities that are not progressing. It is used to highlight activities that are stuck or blocked, and to escalate decisions or action on those items.
- *Backlog* is a prioritized list of work items that need to be done, on which work has not yet begun. It may appear in a table, or on a project board.

Agile reports are typically issued monthly and bi-weekly, and on-demand for specific meetings. The stakeholder audience is often limited to the project sponsor, project and organizational executives, program and project managers, and project team members within the PMO, but may include governing boards, government agencies, financiers, and insurers.

Burndown

A burndown chart shows the amount of effort required to complete a scope of work or list of tasks, represented as a line chart. The end point of the burndown line, where it intersects the x-axis, is the estimated completion date for the work. A typical burndown report compares projected against actual burndown.

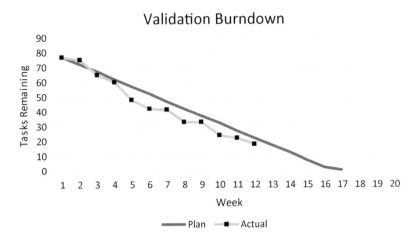

Figure 5.32 Burndown chart example.

The burndown chart shown above plots actual vs. planned task completions per week.

A *burnup report* shows essentially the same data as the burndown chart, with the addition of a line depicting changes in the scope of work.

The burnup report shown below shows the total scope each week, with a separate line for task completions. The report uses the same data as in Figure 5.32 – the Burndown chart example shown above, except the scope changes are more visible.

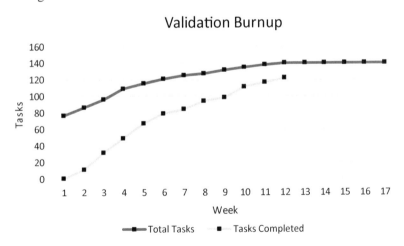

Figure 5.33 Burnup chart example.

Throughput

A throughput report describes the number of work units delivered over time, measured periodically. Summary metrics may be included, such as average work units, a total of work units accepted and completed to date, and additional statistics. The statistical information can be used to predict how many work units the project team can process in future periods. The difference between input and output in the throughput graphic is the work item backlog.

The cycle time graphic below shows the number of activities received each week, and the number of activities completed. The data set graphed is the same as that used in Figure 5.32 – the Burndown chart example; Figure 5.33 – the Burnup chart example; Figure 5.35 – the Cumulative flow example, and Figure 4.7 – the Stacked bar chart.

Note that the statistics in a throughput report do not include information on the size of each work item; this is the primary difference between a throughput report and a velocity report. A *velocity report* graphically represents the amount of value delivered per sprint, by comparing commitments to work completed.

Cumulative flow

A cumulative flow diagram is an area chart that is used to visualize work in progress (WIP), indicating progress in workflow by comparing planned,

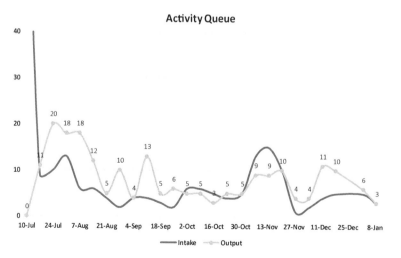

Figure 5.34 Throughput example.

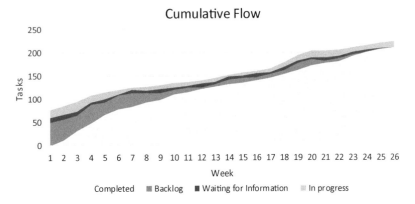

Figure 5.35 Cumulative flow example.

in progress, and completed work over time. It is, essentially, a combination of data seen in the burnup, in progress, and backlog reports. The angle of curves on a cumulative flow diagram indicates throughput.

The cumulative flow example below shows the status of various tasks by category per week, while also illustrating progress made (tasks completed). The data set graphed is the same as that used in Figure 4.6 – the Stacked bar chart.

Cycle time

A cycle time report illustrates how long it takes for work to be completed, usually measured in days, and is often discussed in the context of work in progress. Summary metrics may be included, such as average cycle time, a total of work items completed to date, and additional statistics. Cycle time is a lagging indicator of flow.

The stacked bar chart shown below (Figure 5.36) displays the cycle time per task, with additional detail about the time required for different stages of the task.

Lead time is similar to cycle time and is also measured in days. It includes the time lag between a request being made (work item identified) and work started on the request, in addition to the time required for the work item to be completed (the time during which the work is truly in progress). That is, lead time considers the amount of time a work item sits on the bench, waiting to be started.

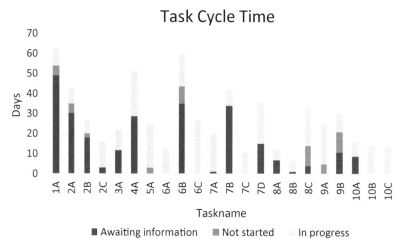

Figure 5.36 Cycle time example.

Special-purpose/ad hoc reports

Funding source

The use of funding from external or internal sources always requires compliance with the terms and conditions by which the transaction is governed. This is especially true for public funding. Examples of funding sources include: funds generated by voter taxes or public bonds, matching funds from a public agency or company, loans, government subsidies, crowdfunding, grants, or donations from a public or private entity. Funding source requirements typically include constraints on the purpose for which the funds may be used, and timing for the expenditure of funds. "Color of money" is a term used to describe the challenges faced by organizations that receive funds from multiple sources, in terms of tracking expenditures, remembering expiration dates, and justifying fund expenditures.

Funding sources have specific reporting requirements, in which accountability and transparency for funds use are of paramount importance, and reporting is required for both expended and remaining funds. For funding source reporting, due dates for reports are inflexible; a missed date may mean withdrawal of funding.

Funding source reports are typically issued monthly and at project milestones, and on-demand for specific meetings. The stakeholder audience is often limited to the project sponsor, project and organizational executives

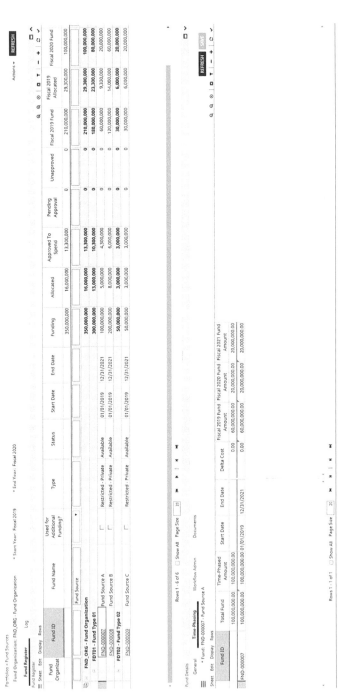

Figure 5.37 Funding sources report example.

Source: Graphic provided by Hexagon, using EcoSys software.

(especially the CFO), program and project managers, and project team members within the PMO, but may include governing boards, government agencies, and financiers.

The funding source report below presents information about funding sources in a tabular format. Data provided includes the funding availability by date, amount available, and amounts allocated. In this example, all three funding sources are being used for one project.

Contractual requirements

Compliance is a review of adherence to certain mandatory requirements, which can be found in the contracts agreed for delivery of the project. Such requirements will typically govern the administration of the contract, milestone deliverables, required documentation to be provided with invoices, approval of invoices and change orders, and more. Of particular importance are report due dates; a missed date may have significant consequences. The report may be as simple as a checklist of items.

Contractual requirement reports are typically issued monthly and at project milestones, and on-demand for specific meetings. The stakeholder audience is often limited to the project sponsor, project and organizational executives, program and project managers, and project team members within the PMO, but may include governing boards, government agencies, and financiers.

Regulatory requirements

Regulatory compliance is often a requirement on projects, and is related to applicable laws, codes, standards, and regulatory/statutory requirements that are mandated by an external agency or authority, or self-imposed by an organization. Regulatory agencies typically have specific reporting requirements and formats. Of particular importance are report due dates; a missed date may have significant consequences for current and future projects. The report may be as simple as a checklist of items, or may be an output from compliance software.

Regulatory compliance reports are typically issued monthly and at project milestones, and on-demand for specific meetings. The stakeholder audience is often limited to the project sponsor, project and organizational executives, program and project managers, and project team members within the PMO, but may include governing boards, government agencies, financiers, and insurers.

Claims

A claim is a request for contract adjustment that has not been resolved through other mechanisms such as change orders. Claims resolution is a legal process. Key to understanding and resolving claims is the contract, along with various types of analysis (such as schedule impact, cost impact, productivity, and root cause). Timing of claims submission is of particular importance when the contract stipulates such requirements; a missed date may mean rejection of the claim. Previously described reports, such as daily project reports, project status reports, change orders, and more, are substantiating documentation for claims.

A claims report will typically list all claims on the project and their status (open, pending, closed), and various descriptive statistics such as dates opened and closed, amount claimed, validated amount, and categorization. The report is similar to an issue resolution report, with some restrictions due to attorney–client privilege.

Claims reports are issued monthly, and on-demand for specific meetings. Due to the highly sensitive nature of the information, the stakeholder audience is typically limited to the project sponsor, project and organizational executives (especially the OGC), and select program and project managers.

Safety

On many projects that require physical labor or human interaction, a safety policy will govern expectations and policies. This will typically include drug-free and alcohol-free rules at the workplace, safety training and orientations, inspections of major equipment and safety gear, personal protective equipment (PPE), emergency procedures, housekeeping, hazard communication, and incentive programs. Safety reporting will typically focus on statistics regarding compliance, safe work hours, injuries (lost-time, recordable, and non-recordables/near-misses), and project safety activities, with a goal of zero accidents. The statistics may have additional granularity by contractor and subcontractor, and type of injury. A project safety report may be required at project closeout, which includes not only the statistical data but also lessons learned. Safety reporting may be narrative, and often includes dashboard or infographic elements.

Safety reports are typically issued monthly and at project milestones, and on-demand for specific meetings. The stakeholder audience is often limited to the project sponsor, project and organizational executives, program and project managers, and project team members within the PMO, but may include governing boards, contractors, government agencies, financiers, and insurers.

Testing and inspection

In accordance with project requirements and regulations, certain tests and inspections will be conducted and reported during the course of the project. Testing and inspection reporting will typically focus on a summary of work, statistics regarding testing and inspection results, and written observations and recommendations regarding nonconformances. Timing and format may depend on external regulations.

Testing and inspection reports are issued on an ad hoc basis. The stakeholder audience is often limited to the program and project managers, and project team members within the PMO, but may include other interested parties if the reports identify risks and quality issues.

Sustainability

On a project, sustainability reporting may relay information about energy consumption, environmental and social impact, cultural heritage, wildlife conservation and biodiversity, carbon footprint, building certifications, mitigation and enhancement measures to protect all the above, and more. Sustainability reporting will typically include actions taken and statistics. It may utilize a checklist to indicate compliance. The report may follow a prescribed framework.

A sustainability report is often issued on an annual basis and at the end of the project, but may also be produced more frequently and on-demand for specific meetings. Internal stakeholders interested in a sustainability report may include: governing boards, the project or program sponsor, project and organizational executives, and the program and project manager. External stakeholders include regulatory, licensing, and government agencies, financiers and insurers, and the general public.

Press releases

A press release is an official announcement from the project or owner organization, usually written by a public relations department. For public-facing projects, major events/milestones, product launch, and more, these news announcements are a way to capture the attention of the general public and prospective customers, using the press and social media as a distribution mechanism. Press releases tend to have a very specific format, and are fairly succinct and simply worded, with a headline, lede, quotes, and contact information.

Press releases are often issued at project milestones and on an ad hoc basis. Their audience includes all internal and external stakeholders, especially the general public.

6   Challenges

As much as the project team might want on-demand real-time reporting at the push of a button, the reality is that project data comes from many sources, and that causes a number of challenges when producing project reports. The reliability of data used to manage a project is extremely important, and the keys to reliability are dependability, accuracy, and timeliness. Chapter 6 – Challenges, discusses some of the obstacles and issues typically encountered when developing project reports, and ways to overcome them.

Systems integration

Each of the data systems mentioned earlier may have its own code of accounts and specific timing for data receipt and entry, making it difficult for the project team to fully integrate all the databases and systems needed to generate dependable, timely, and accurate project reports. Some of the challenges with systems integration are discussed below.

Paper-based information

It is almost impossible for the typical project team to avoid paper-based documentation, and the information contained therein. Admittedly, it is burdensome for projects to rely on and receive paper documents, but it is in many situations made necessary by organizational processes and internal or external requirements. Information received in this fashion will result in the need for project team members to scan or manually enter data into the project management system of record, if possible. Challenges with manual data entry include the time required to enter information, and risks of duplication and human error.

Examples of paper-based documentation may include:

- Invoices
- Receipts

- Checks and cancelled checks
- Credit card statements
- Posted letters
- Facsimiles (increasingly rare)
- Government documentation
- Legal documents
- Timesheets
- Goods received notes
- Output from testing

External data

Some project information will be received from external sources that are completely disconnected from the project management system and other organizational systems. Again, this results in a need for project team members to manually enter data. Challenges with external data include verification of accuracy and reliability, along with the above-mentioned issues with manual data entry.

External data sources include but are not limited to:

- Weather reports
- Websites
- News reports
- Voicemail
- Photographic records
- Benchmarked data
- Inflation data
- Currency fluctuations

Coding

Project, activity, and resource coding may differ between the various systems and databases used to produce data for project reports. In order to reliably access the correct data, the various data sources need to be mapped to each other, ensuring horizontal traceability and an apples-to-apples matching of information across systems.

Once an initial mapping exercise is completed, data validation is typically achieved by reconciling all systems. When all fields and codes have been matched up, reports from various systems can easily be produced and compared as needed. Data conflicts, discrepancies between reports, and exception reports can then be used to identify and correct miscoded cost data and cost allocations to project accounts. If the project team has not created a coding map for various systems, the capture of information for reports will be a tedious exercise potentially fraught with errors, each and every time a report is produced.

Bridges

Custom programming is still a reality and requirement when developing integrated reporting that pulls information from multiple systems. Bridges are typically used to enable accounting, ERP, project management, and other legacy systems to "talk" to each other, filling in gaps in information transfer and enabling interoperability between systems. It is possible to create automated routines to mine information from different systems, such as an ETL (extract, transfer, and load) routine, capturing various kinds information that are subsequently stored in a data warehouse, and accessed as needed to produce project reports. Such routines are run periodically, refreshing data so the information available is always up-to-date. Automating the data-pull and data migration exercise may reduce the potential for human error when entering and assembling information for project reports, and eliminate the need for dual-entry.

Lack of a bridge or systems integration will result in the need for project team members to manually compile and enter data from multiple sources, and transform information into the necessary format for reports. Such an effort is very labor intensive and inefficient, can require a significant amount of time, and can result in human error.

Level of detail

A particular challenge occurs when working with contractors to access data from their systems of record. Contractors work with many clients, and their cost codes are structured to suit their own organizational needs, not those of their clients. If the accounting structure utilized by the contractor does not enable the reporting of information in a WBS and at the level of detail required by the contract, the contractor will be perpetually delinquent in satisfying the requirements of the contract, significantly violating contract terms. If the contractor's system is unable to provide sufficient detail, it may effectively hide areas of project risk.

Similarly, accounting systems may allow only one entry per purchase order, whereas the project team requires more granularity of data for large or long-lead equipment, and other individual line items within the purchase order. In such instances, the project team will need to access the original purchase order and enter the line items into the project system of record.

Accuracy

Confidence in project data and reporting is paramount, yet data may be biased, misrepresented, missing, incomplete, out of date, or just incorrect, whether intentionally or unintentionally. Systems integration can solve some of those problems, but not all. Validation and reconciliation of data are two methods of ensuring data and report accuracy.

Validation

Mentioned above as part of systems mapping and coding, data validation is a primary mechanism of data cleansing to ensure the quality, integrity, accuracy, and consistency of systems data. In terms of project data, validation is the process of checking the fitness and completeness of data, and tracing data to its source. Project team members may develop their own spreadsheets, to supplement electronic validation. Validation may also be conducted as part of a quality assurance/quality control process for calculations and modeling.

Reconciliation

Where there is system redundancy, whereby the same information appears in multiple systems, those systems need to be reconciled regularly to identify and correct errors and omissions. Reconciliation may be part of the validation process, described above. It is useful in identifying mismatches between systems, missing records, incorrect data, duplicated records, and human error.

Timeliness

Timeliness of data, regularity in the availability of reports, and punctuality in the provision of information are incredibly important in project management. Late information means late decision-making, or assumptions made that lead to incorrect decisions. However, a common challenge in project management is the ability of the project team to access and integrate information in a timely fashion. Project reporting may even have a domino effect of lateness, wherein lateness of data and reports that are used as input to a comprehensive dashboard or monthly status report have a negative impact on the timeliness of subsequent reports.

Late information

There is, inevitably, some lag time between data receipt, input, and reporting. Delays in reporting are caused by overdue approvals (such as contracts and change orders), manual data entry, difficulties in gathering and entering data, efforts to validate information, and the complexities of assembling, formatting, and generating project reports. This is most true for comprehensive reports and dashboards, but is also true in any instance where pre-formatted and pre-populated reports are not generated automatically from an electronic project management system. Systems integration can solve some timeliness problems, but not all.

Data cut-off dates

Another timeliness challenge is the possibility of inconsistency between systems regarding data cut-off dates. For each management system, reporting periods are typically defined, which require a datacut. Typical cut-off dates are the end of the month and end of the year. Problems with datacuts include partial dates (where date information is incomplete), and data received after the cut-off (see discussion above, late information). There is usually a lag between the data cut-off and the date of the report, due to the aforementioned challenges of assembling, formatting, and generating project reports. Consistency in data cut-off dates is imperative when generating project metrics, such as measuring production within a fixed time period, and mapping cash flow.

Accountability

Transparency

While public disclosure of project data may be required, voluntary disclosure of information on private projects is increasing in response to requests from stakeholders and a trend toward self-regulation. Transparency on projects is not limited to status and performance; it can extend to decision-making, authorizations, risk, change, and more. Transparency is a means of ensuring accountability, and encourages responsible action by project team members.

Bias

Optimism bias occurs when the project team knowingly (or, more likely, unknowingly) reports more favorable conditions than are realistic. Project teams constantly underestimate the likelihood of change, and are subject to planning fallacies wherein they overestimate progress. Such bias originates in overconfidence in the project team or market conditions, a cognitive illusion of invulnerability, perceived control, wishful thinking, and underestimation of risk. It can lead to poor decision-making, especially when it results in reluctance to terminate or significantly redesign a failing project.

Pessimism bias, although considerably less common, may also occur. Pessimism bias occurs when a project report exaggerates the poor performance, complexity, and risk of the project. This may be done by a project team member in order to express concern, receive additional resources for the project, or to sandbag results so as to appear more accomplished at a later point in time.

With anchoring bias, an unreasonable or excessive weight is given to a previously reported value or preconceived ideas. Anchoring often occurs on projects with respect to finish dates and initial budgetary amounts, even if those values were highly conceptual and elicited many years in the past (thus no longer relevant). Stakeholders can be highly susceptible to anchoring bias. Availability bias is a tendency to rely on statistics and information that are easy to remember; it may be a type of anchoring bias, along with hindsight bias.

Personal bias may be more correctable than optimism and pessimism bias, as input from multiple individuals can normalize an opinionated outlier. Personal bias can impact a project in many ways, not the least of which are the selection and prioritization of projects, risk modeling, and project status reporting. Project teams are also influenced by sunk costs and groupthink (or herding behavior). Confirmation bias is a tendency to collect evidence that confirms a particular belief, ignoring evidence to the contrary or treating it with extreme skepticism, and may be a type of personal bias or fixation, along with mere exposure effect. This is where a quality control/quality assurance process will benefit the project, by providing tiers of review of workproduct.

Expert opinion

Expert opinion is an oft-required input in project management and project controls systems, such as risk quantification, schedule durations, forecasting, and estimating. Experts rely heavily on judgment and experience, when ideating project data. Experts exist and are a necessity because not all project data is easily acquired, or even available; not every piece of information on a project is an absolute, Platonic truth. They are a class of project participants that have private knowledge, and there is a fallacy in the assumption that because they have expertise, certification, and training they are qualified in all circumstances. Experts make the project team, stakeholders, and other non-specialists feel better about uncertainty. They fill a gap. It is hoped they will utilize best available evidence, curate information appropriately, and document their assumptions. However, experts have varying levels of tolerance for risk, and are not immune to bias and advocacy. As such, expert opinions can vary quite dramatically. Further, if the expert is internal to the project team, their opinion might not be independent and objective. Expert input should be utilized on the project with discretion, and regarded with care.

Qualitative data

Projects capture both quantitative and qualitative data. Quantitative data is easy to verify, and is often accompanied by supporting documentation. Qualitative data is usually narrative and text-based in format, and received from many sources.

Origins of qualitative data may include:

- Needs assessments
- Incoming reports
- Observation records
- Drawings
- Meeting minutes and transcripts
- Surveys and questionnaires
- Interviews
- Correspondence
- Notes and diaries

A primary challenge with qualitative data is that it tends to contain opinions in addition to facts. Some qualitative data can be supported by evidence; some cannot. It may be difficult to parse. Qualitative information often represents an individual's experience or view of the project and may be subject to various types of bias, as discussed above. Care should be taken when using qualitative data, and supporting documentation obtained when possible.

Traceability

As mentioned above, with expert opinion and qualitative data, traceability of data to its source is a form of transparency. All data should be supported by calculations and source information, and assumptions documented.

Even if the data is commonly known among the project team, it is important to capture background information and store it for future retrieval, when the project is finished and the organization can no longer pursue the project team with questions. Project outputs regularly outlive project team members.

Selective reporting

Critical project problems may be deliberately concealed, especially in an organizational culture that discourages the reporting of bad news, or where performance is tied to rewards. Information may be omitted, selectively featured, reclassified, and more, all in an effort to portray project status more favorably. Schedule and cost may be re-baselined, to obfuscate change from the original plan. Even if issues are reported by the project team, they may be downplayed by project executives who are reluctant to hear bad news, known as the "deaf effect." Entire reports may even be withheld from distribution.

Issues with flow and availability of project information are an indicator of problems on the project; selective reporting conceals change and risk, misrepresenting the true status of the project. Small changes, such as cost increases and schedule delays, might not be reported by the project team, either dismissed as immaterial, or not divulged in the hope the changes can be reversed. This prevents early action to mitigate the issues, and may even delay reporting and escalation of issues until they are too great to ignore and cannot be remedied. Studies of project reports[1] indicate a pervasive tendency toward both optimism bias in reports and selective reporting, in which certain information is omitted because it does not contribute toward a positive perception of the project. In such studies, results show that project status reports are often believed to be incomplete and less than credible.[2] Not only do doctored project status reports reduce faith and trust in reporting, they also withhold accurate information from decision makers, effectively further damaging the project through the concealment of risk and increasing the likelihood of project failure. Probability of project failure or poor performance is often well known by project team members, and numerous warning signs noted, long before such information is reported and appropriate action taken.

Misuse of reports

As mentioned earlier, most reports are designed for a specific stakeholder audience. Once generated, the information contained in most project reports can be considered common knowledge that is shared among internal and external stakeholders. When used by other parties to make decisions, such summaries of management information and aggregate data can be potentially dangerous.

Selective reporting may occur if the project team does not trust the intended audience for the report. Potential misuse and release of information is a project risk the team well understands, and the project team may be motivated to protect the project by withholding information, creating knowledge silos in the project organization.

Ethics

There exists the question of whether whistleblowing should be required of the project team, should project reports be inaccurate, overly optimistic, or withheld from distribution. Key to this question are decisions about whether or not the offense is egregious enough to warrant reportage, frequency of occurrence, organizational culture, who should be responsible for that action, and what repercussions will likely result. The creation of processes and pathways for whistleblowing, such as an anonymous hotline and whistleblower protections, will also increase the likelihood of occurrence.

There are a number of issues and complications with the concept of whistleblowing. First, where optimism bias exists, the project team may fully, if irrationally, believe they can achieve significant performance improvements during the next reporting cycle. In such an instance, the perception of wrongdoing, urgency, and potential impact may be quite low, which would deter the reportage of bias and/or inaccuracies. Second, the inclination to report bias and/or inaccuracies may vary according to whether the report is internal or external. Certain external reports, such as those to the media, and customers, may contain "spin" to make the situation appear more attractive, or may report the minimum required amount of detail in order to reduce public scrutiny or comment. The inclination to report bias and/or inaccuracies, in such a situation, will likely depend on whether the report is considered to be completely false instead of merely slanted, the potential implications, and the individual's concepts of justice and fairness. This is especially true where public safety is a factor. Other external reports (such as regulatory and financial reports) are more critical to the organization, and individuals may feel an obligation or duty to report bias and/or inaccuracies for such official and mandatory reports.

Notes

1 Iacovou, Charalambos L., Thompson, Ronald L., and Smith, J. Jeff (2009). Selective Status Reporting in Information Systems Projects: A Dyadic-Level Investigation. *MIS Quarterly*, 33(4), pp. 785–810. Minneapolis, MN: Management Information Systems Research Center, University of Minnesota.
2 Thompson, Ronald L., Smith, H. Jeff, and Iacovou, Charalambos L. (2007). The Linkage Between Reporting Quality and Performance in IS Projects. *Information & Management*, 44(2), pp. 196–205. Amsterdam, Netherlands: Elsevier.

7   Summary

No matter how much project management evolves and progresses, communication with internal and external stakeholders will continue to be a vital part of the project process. Report styles will ebb and flow in popularity, the methods used to generate them will certainly change, and the systems used to collect, manage, and analyze data will no doubt become more sophisticated and integrated. Advancements in technology will undoubtedly make an impact on the reporting capabilities of the project team.

As mentioned earlier, the report itself is less important than the decisions that form project outcomes; it is, however, an indispensable vehicle for decision-making and contributes to the project's permanent record. Stakeholders will always rely heavily on qualitative and quantitative information in order to make decisions.

The future

The future of project reporting is not all that different from the present, in terms of the types of information measured and reported. The difference is in the technology used to do so, and the power of data and analytics. To some degree, the future is already here; predictive analytics and machine learning are already available to some project teams. In the immediate future, the power and proliferation of such tools will continue to increase. The hope, of course, is that the future of project reporting will be able to counteract, overcome, and even prevent the many challenges and obstacles described earlier.

Predictive analytics

Developments in modeling and data mining are enabling more sophisticated types of statistical analysis that reach considerably beyond traditional descriptive analytics and business intelligence. These more advanced techniques, such as predictive and prescriptive analytics, leverage computing power and data mining to help to identify relationships and patterns in a collection of data, and calculate statistical probabilities. The data may be historical, or transactional. Not only does this theoretically enable better forecasting, assessment of risk, and diagnosis of project problems, the analytics are expected to improve as more data is entered into the system over time, using historic information and insight as inputs to make more accurate predictions. Improved analytics mean better decision models, and thus better decision-making.

In the graphic below, the software draws on schedule data to identify and manage risks and opportunities.

Predictive analytics are not limited to numeric analysis. The same techniques can be applied to unstructured (text) data, extracting patterns and meaning from project documents and written feedback. This can be used to identify inconsistencies and potential risks.

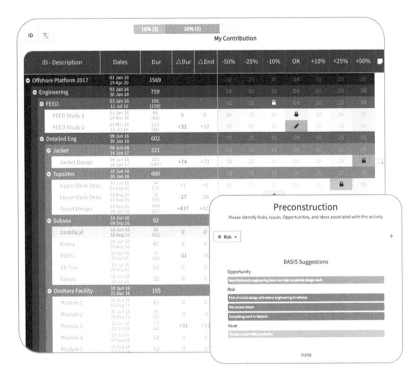

Figure 7.1 Predictive analytics example.

Source: Graphic provided by InEight, using InEight Basis software.

The challenge with any type of analytics, even today, is the pervasive problem of quality and quantity of data. Garbage-in/garbage-out is one way of describing problems with data quality, which will persist. Forecasts and predictions made using incorrect, inactionable, inappropriate, or incomplete data will, naturally, yield forecasts and predictions that are incorrect, inactionable, inappropriate and/or arguably incomplete.

Quantity of data was discussed earlier in this book, in the context of project forecasting and trending, and it is also true in the practice of predictive analytics. A minimum of two data points are needed to draw a trend line and create a forecast, but the quality of the predictive model increases with the quantity of data points provided, increasing confidence with each addition. As internet of things (IoT) technology proliferates on projects, increasing the number of data-capturing devices and sensors, the amount of available data should increase.

Machine learning

Beyond mere analytics, the next generation of technology uses learning data representations (machine learning) at various levels of abstraction to mimic the complexities of human thought processes and draw conclusions from data. The foundations of learning algorithms include representation (classification), evaluation (scoring), and optimization. There are many potential uses of this machine learning technology. It can:

- Interpolate data (identifying and filling in data gaps);
- Be trained to recognize potentially bad data, and even prompt the project team to effect improvements to the quality of gathered data;
- Collect project metadata, setting the stage for new types of project analytics;
- Design project processes;
- Automate project planning and resource leveling;
- Generate a preliminary project budget and/or schedule;
- Perform nonlinear modeling of complex functions for prediction, classification, and control;
- Approximate common-sense decision-making.

Of course, the same challenges currently exist with quality and quantity of data, and those challenges may even be compounded in a butterfly effect when that data is utilized by artificial intelligence in a cascade of nonlinear processing. A system that learns from bad data is not a useful system at all. This means the project can welcome artificial intelligence (AI) to the team, but must be prepared to supervise data cleansing and machine learning, and validate, vet, and fact-check its output.

One benefit of advancements in machine learning will be a reduction in the amount of available data needed for modeling. This will greatly benefit users who have historically lacked the volume of data needed to use early-adopter intelligent systems.

Closing comments

This book is intended to serve several purposes. It offers some guidance regarding data sources for reports, report audiences, and common pitfalls in reporting. It also offers a wealth of examples of different types of reports. Together, the book is crafted to be a valuable resource for any organization or project team that wants to communicate more effectively with internal and/or external stakeholders. It advocates a carefully considered approach to crafting project reports, which will increase the likelihood of identifying and acting on project issues and risks, thus improving project performance.

The author hopes this contribution to the body of knowledge for project reporting will result in greater maturity in project communication, and better awareness of the intent and variability in types of project reports. Ultimately, deeper understanding of reporting as a project management best practice may lead to new developments in predictive analytics and machine learning, resulting in even better data analysis and reporting. It is also hoped that this book will lead to improved recognition and prestige of project management and related professions.

Additional resources

Published works by the author

Nalewaik, Alexia and Mills, Anthony (2016). *Project Performance Review: Capturing the Value of Audit, Oversight, and Compliance for Project Success.* London: Routledge.

Nalewaik, Alexia and Witt, Jeffrey (2010). Challenges Reporting Project Costs and Risks to Owner Decisionmakers. *Cost Engineering*, August. Morgantown, WV: AACE International.

Other recommended reading

Besner, Claude and Hobbs, J. Brian (2010). An empirical identification of project management toolsets and a comparison among project types. *2010 PMI® Research Conference: Defining the Future of Project Management.* Newtown Square, PA: Project Management Institute.

Blodgett, John W. and Criss, Brian (2014). Integrated Project Reporting Using Dashboards: Harnessing the Power of Primavera P6. *2014 AACE International Transactions.* Morgantown, WV: AACE International.

Keil, Mark, Smith, H. Jeff, Iacovou, Charalambos L., and Thompson, Ronald L. (2014). The Pitfalls of Project Status Reporting. *MIT Sloan Management Review*, 55(3), pp. 57–64. Cambridge, MA: Massachusetts Institution of Technology.

Mohanani, Rahul, Salman, Iflaah, Turhan, Burak, Rodriguez, Pilar, and Ralph, Paul (October 2018). Cognitive Biases in Software Engineering: A Systematic Mapping and Quasi-Literature Review. *IEEE Transactions on Software Engineering.* Piscataway, NJ: Institute of Electrical and Electronics Engineers.

Smith, H. Jeff, Keil, Mark, and Depledge, Gordon (2001). Keeping Mum as the Project Goes Under: Toward an Explanatory Model. *Journal of Management Information Systems*, 18(2), pp. 189–227. London: Taylor & Francis.

Virine, Lev, Trumper, Michael, and Virine, Eugenia (April 2018). Event Chain Diagrams. *PM World Journal*, 7(4). Addison, TX: PM World Inc.

Waples, Christopher J., and Culbertson, Satoris S. (2011). Best-Laid Plans: Can Whistleblowing on Project Problems Be Encouraged? *Academy of Management Perspectives*, 25(2), pp. 80–82. Briarcliff Manor, NY: Academy of Management.

Index